The Mycenaeans
c. 1650–1100 BC

Nicolas Grguric · Illustrated by Angus McBride

Consultant editor Martin Windrow

First published in Great Britain in 2005 by Osprey Publishing,
Midland House, West Way, Botley, Oxford OX2 0PH, UK
443 Park Avenue South, New York, NY 10016, USA
Email: info@ospreypublishing.com

ISBN 1 84176 897 9

Page layouts by Ken Vail Graphic Design, Cambridge, UK
Index by Alison Worthington
Originated by The Electronic Page Company, Cwmbran, UK
Printed in China through World Print Ltd.

05 06 07 08 09   10 9 8 7 6 5 4 3 2 1

A CIP catalogue record for this book
is available from the British Library

FOR A CATALOGUE OF ALL BOOKS PUBLISHED BY
OSPREY MILITARY AND AVIATION PLEASE CONTACT:

North America:
Osprey Direct
2427 Bond Street, University Park, IL 60466, USA
Email: info@ospreydirectusa.com

All other regions:
Osprey Direct UK
PO Box 140, Wellingborough, Northants NN8 2FA, UK
Email: info@ospreydirect.co.uk

Buy online at **www.ospreypublishing.com**

Acknowledgements

First and foremost the author would like to thank Michael
Kumnick, without whose artistic skill the briefings for Angus
McBride's striking colour plates would not have been
possible, and for putting up with my nit-picking. Thanks
also go to Dr Margaret O'Hea of the University of Adelaide,
who supported and supervised my research on this topic as
an Honours student; to Prof Dr Hans-Günther Buchholz for
granting permission to use many of his own images; to the
Hellenic Ministry of Culture; and to my family.

Artist's Note

Readers may care to note that the original paintings from
which the colour plates in this book were prepared are
available for private sale. All reproduction copyright
whatsoever is retained by the Publishers. All enquiries
should be addressed to:

Scorpio Gallery,
PO Box 475,
Hailsham,
E.Sussex
BN27 2SL,
UK

The Publishers regret that they can enter into no
correspondence upon this matter.

THE MYCENAEANS
c.1650–1180 BC

INTRODUCTION

The Mycenaean civilization spanned a period of 400–500 years, from the early 16th century BC until its decline in the 12th century BC. During this time it evolved from the role of envious admirer of the more advanced Minoan civilization based on nearby Crete, into a civilization whose power and influence eclipsed that of the Minoans and dominated Greece and the Aegean.

'The Mycenaeans' is not a designation that would have been recognized by the Classical authors. To the Greeks, their earliest ancestors were referred to variously as 'Achaeans', 'Danaans' and 'Argives'. These were terms that came down to them through epic poetry and numerous legends, which were often contradictory. Indeed, this period remained in the realm of legend until the late 19th century AD, when Heinrich Schliemann, in search of treasure and physical proof of Homer's Trojan War, began excavating the site of Mycenae, which Homer says was the seat of King Agamemnon.

Just inside the citadel's gates Schliemann unearthed several burials which, to judge by their wealth, belonged to the highest class of Mycenaean society. These burials contained a wealth of grave goods of gold, silver, bronze, ivory and ceramic – with gold predominating. Schliemann interpreted these burials as the mortal remains of the heroes of Homer's epics. In this he was mistaken; what he did not know at the time was that he had unearthed the tombs of a dynasty that reigned some 300 years before the supposed date of the Trojan War (c.1260–1250 BC).[1] Although Schliemann's identifications were at fault, he rightly claimed that he had discovered a new world for archaeology. Through his enterprise a forgotten civilization was reborn, and took its name from this city.

Later research and excavation showed that this civilization pervaded not only the Greek mainland but the Aegean islands and countries bordering on the central and eastern Mediterranean. Many more sites were found in this region, displaying the same cultural characteristics as Mycenae – similar architectural styles, art, pottery, language, religion, and weapons. Several of these were

Steatite cup from the Cretan palace of Hagia Triada, 16th century BC. It shows some elements of Cretan military equipment subsequently adopted by the Mycenaeans, such as the long thrusting sword and, just visible at the left, part of a 'tower' shield. (Courtesy of the Heraclion Museum)

1 See Osprey, Fortress 17, *Troy c.1700–1250 BC*

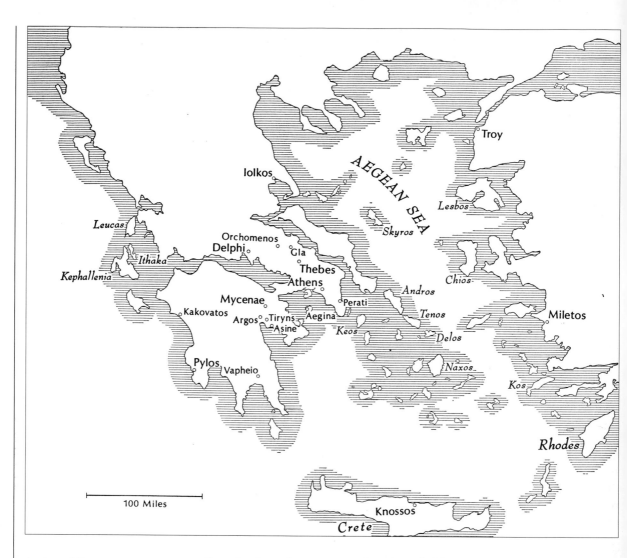

Centres of Mycenaean civilization. (George Mylonas, *Mycenae and the Mycenaean Age*, © 1966 Princeton University Press; reprinted by permission of Princeton University Press)

found to have been great palace-based cities on a scale rivalling Mycenae itself, such as Tiryns and Pylos in the Mycenaean heartland of the Peloponnese, which were established around 1650 BC.

Emergence of Mycenae

The early history of the Mycenaean period is notable for its penchant for all things Minoan. The Minoan civilization of Crete can be traced as far back as c.3000 BC; it therefore had more time to develop its culture than the mainlanders, helped to a large extent by close interaction with surrounding civilizations in the form of seaborne trading. The Minoan character of early Mycenaean art is so marked that it led some to believe that the southern part of Greece must have been a Cretan colony. It has since become apparent that this similarity was the result of influence rather than colonization. One distinct area of Minoan influence on the Mycenaeans was that of warfare; indeed, most of the early weapon and armour types that are characteristic of the Mycenaeans actually originated on Minoan Crete. One notable exception is the chariot, however, which appears to have been introduced on to Crete by the Mycenaeans rather than the other way around.

The earlier Minoan culture was not Greek, and wrote using an as yet undeciphered syllabic script called Linear A. The Mycenaeans, however, were Greek, as was demonstrated by the decipherment of their script known as Linear B. The language of this script is an early form of Greek, showing that the history of Mycenaean culture is both geographically and ethnically part of the history of Greece. The Linear B script comes to us in the form of small clay tablets mostly found in the ruins of the palaces, the most informative coming from Pylos and Mycenaean Knossos. The subject matter of these tablets is not narrative but bureaucratic: that is, they record the daily business of the palace-based society and economy. Some of these tablets record aspects of the military organization of the palace-state, and have provided an important source of information about the Mycenaean army.

Mycenaean dominance
In around 1400 BC the centre of Minoan power on Crete, Knossos, was destroyed, probably by an earthquake. It seems that the Mycenaeans of mainland Greece took advantage of this disaster to take over Crete; they rebuilt Knossos as a Mycenaean palace, and Crete became a Mycenaean kingdom. With the removal of its main rival, Mycenaean civilization became the dominant cultural power in the Aegean. The Mycenaeans used their regional dominance to expand their trading networks and developed close contacts with surrounding civilizations, notably those of the Near East such as the Hittites, Syrians and Egyptians. There is even evidence that the Egyptian and Mycenaean armies employed each other's troops as mercenaries. Although there is evidence that the Mycenaeans sent an expeditionary force to the coast of Anatolia (modern Turkey) to fight the Hittites, their usual enemies were most likely competing palace-states, and 'barbarians' from the less controlled regions of Greece. At times Mycenaean palace-states seem to have formed confederations, as described in Homer's *Iliad*.

The evidence: Homer, and the archaeological record
The works of poetry attributed to Homer have always been closely associated with the study of Mycenaean history, and their relationship with the evidence that comes down to us from the Mycenaean period should be understood. Although Homer's epics are tentatively set in the Mycenaean period, it is generally believed that these stories originated much later, in around the 8th century BC, some 300 years after the end of the Mycenaean civilization and during Greece's 'Dark Age'. Where accurate references to the Mycenaean period are found in Homer, these must be the result of folklore preserved via oral history. However, as an historical record of the Mycenaean civilization and of Mycenaean warfare the great poet's writings have limited value. This is because the accurately remembered elements were combined with inventions and post-Mycenaean elements, as well as much later inclusions and adaptations from the Classical period and later.

What we know of the Mycenaean army – a term used in this text for brevity, to mean all armies of that broad civilization, across their whole timespan – comes to us almost entirely through archaeology. The sources of such archaeological evidence as we have include pictorial survivals, e.g. wall paintings; gravestones; precious objects; textual sources in the form of the Linear B tablets; and finds of actual weapons and equipment. Compared to contemporary civilizations such as the Egyptians and Hittites, this overall body of evidence is very limited, the pictorial evidence is often highly stylized and the textual evidence fragmentary. Nevertheless, it is possible to reconstruct the Mycenaean army in surprising detail from the available evidence. One of the reasons for this is that the evidence we do have covers a wide range of aspects of Mycenaean warriors, from dress and equipment, through formations and tactics, to higher organization and logistics.

There is a distinct lack of secondary information available for the Mycenaean army. This is a conspicuous omission in the study of ancient warfare, given the very militaristic character of Mycenaean culture. As Lord Taylour says in his *The Mycenaeans*, 'It would almost seem as if they loved strife for its own sake'. Previous books on the Mycenaean civilization in general often have a small chapter on warfare and weaponry, but this is usually either little more than a summary of the types of weapons and armour known, or heavily influenced by Homer's heroic images of individual duelling warriors. The characteristic items of the Mycenaean warrior's equipment are always described – such as the boar's-tusk helmet, figure-of-eight shield, and the 'Dendra Cuirass' – but usually little or no attempt is made to discuss where these items fitted into the overall functioning of the Mycenaean army. Articles in academic journals describing Mycenaean artefact forms, such as swords, are also plentiful, but fail to contribute greatly to our understanding of what kind of soldiers used these swords and what their tactical role was. It is only when all of the evidence is observed as a whole that a more complete picture emerges. That picture is of a quite conventional Late Bronze Age army, yet with uniquely Mycenaean characteristics.

THE EVOLUTION OF THE MYCENAEAN ARMY

The earliest weapons known to have been used by the mainland Greeks were slings and bows, with battleaxes and stone maces for hand-to-hand combat. The earliest examples come from the Neolithic and Early Bronze Ages (before about 2150 BC). These weapons suggest a very informal mode of warfare waged by tribal hordes rather than by organized armies. Slings and bows continued to be used throughout the Mycenaean period; but as armies became more organized and formalized during the Middle Bronze Age (between c.2150 and 1550 BC), battleaxes and clubs fell out of use. As bronze-working skills were

These limestone sling stones are evidence for early Greek weaponry. Most such projectiles were made of unfired clay; these particular examples come from Thessaly and date to the Late Neolithic period, that is, before 2500 BC. (Courtesy Professor Dr H-G.Buchholz)

developed these stone weapons were replaced by swords and spears.

The earliest evidence for organized Mycenaean armies comes from the late 16th century BC, and shows a strong Minoan influence which lasted throughout the period. The early army of c.1600 to 1300 BC was composed of a core of heavy spearmen supported by swordsmen, light infantry, skirmishers and heavy chariots. This type of army was well suited to fighting set-piece battles against similarly organized opponents such as rival palace-states. The swordsmen and light infantry were also suited to fighting in rough terrain, so were useful for fighting the 'barbarians' who lived in the mountainous, semi-civilized regions outside Mycenaean control. This military organization, with its mixture of heavy spearmen and chariots and lighter auxiliaries, proved effective for a long period during which the only enemies it faced were of these two types. However, during the 13th century BC the Mycenaean military system underwent a major change in equipment and tactics, the reason for which may have been a factor in the eventual collapse of the civilization.

This new type of army first appears in the archaeological record in the artefacts from the palace at Pylos that are dated to the 13th century BC. Pylos lies in the region of Messenia on the west coast of the Peloponnese. When the palace was excavated between 1939 and 1966, it yielded a large cache of Linear B tablets, and frescoes with a military theme. This evidence portrays a much lighter army with a focus on mobility, and suggests

Ivory plaque from Delos depicting an early period spearman. This clearly shows the three characteristic elements of this troop type: the figure-of-eight shield, boar's-tusk helmet, and spear. (After Taylour, 1972)

more dispersed mêlées. This change in tactical doctrine may reflect an increase in seaborne raids along the Mycenaean coast by foreigners. This new threat was possibly caused by the displacement of large numbers of people due to an increase in natural disasters and war throughout the lands surrounding the Mediterranean at this time. The 13th century BC was the time when many of the Mycenaean centres, Mycenae included, erected huge stone ramparts around their citadels, such fortifications clearly reflecting a fear of impending attack. It was at this time that the military leadership at Pylos issued orders for the deployment of bodies of troops along its coastline to guard against seaborne invaders.

What happened next is unclear, except for the significant fact that soon after these orders were transcribed on to clay tablets Pylos was destroyed, in about 1200 BC. Nearly all of the other Mycenaean centres were also destroyed at around this time. The causes of this period of destruction are still a topic of debate amongst scholars. Some possible explanations are that it was caused by warfare, natural disasters, social revolution or a combination of these factors. Some of the cities were rebuilt and reoccupied, but the Mycenaean civilization as it had

Ivory rendition of a figure-of-eight shield. This piece measures 14.3cm × 9.5cm and may have been attached to a piece of furniture or used as a door handle. Such ivory miniatures are the only three-dimensional representations of these shields that we have. This piece dates from the 13th century BC, when the figure-of-eight shield had fallen from actual use but survived as a religious or decorative motif. (Courtesy National Archaeological Museum, Athens)

previously been known was gone. Greece descended into a dark age, her eventual emergence from which is now known as the Classical period.

IDENTIFIABLE CATEGORIES OF TROOPS

HEAVY INFANTRY

The backbone of a Mycenaean army was its heavy infantry. In the early period (c.1650–1300 BC) they were armed with a long spear (*enkhos*) as their main weapon, and a sword. Clothing was minimal, consisting only of a cloth kilt or loincloth, and warriors went barefoot; however, this lack of body armour was compensated for by a large shield (*sakos*) which covered the body from neck to shins, as well as a helmet.

The identification of this type of warrior as a heavy infantryman comes from an analysis of the practical implications of his armour and

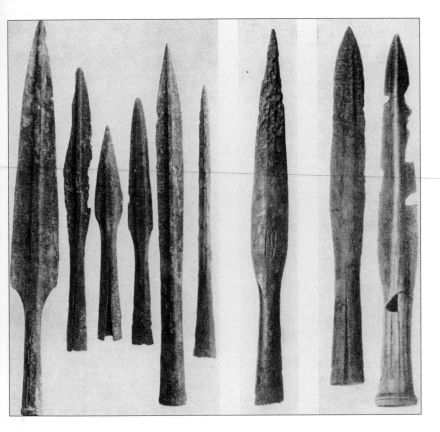

A selection of socketed spearheads from the Mycenaean world. Three are of the slit-socketed type, which were easier to make than the fully developed socketed type. (Courtesy Professor HG.Buchholz, and the British Museum)

weaponry. This type of soldier fought in the typical heavy infantry manner, whose fundamental characteristics are that he fights 'shoulder to shoulder' in compact, massed formations. That these Mycenaean warriors fought in such formations is strongly suggested by their equipment as well as by depictions.

Shields

One of the most diagnostic signs of a heavy infantryman is his shield. This, in both of its patterns (i.e. 'figure-of-eight' and 'tower' shields), protects the body from neck to foot. These shields appear to have been made of wickerwork upon a wooden frame; they were faced with one or more layers of hide, as can be seen in several coloured depictions of them from frescoes. They were carried by means of a *telamon*, a strap which passed over the left shoulder diagonally. Thus supported, the shield left both hands free. Such a large shield tells us specific things about its function. The warrior would have been very well protected from all manner of spear and sword thrusts, javelins, arrows, sling-shots,

Drawing of a 'shoe-socketed' spearhead, with recesses either side of the blade into which a split shaft was fixed. This was the predecessor of the socketed spearhead proper. (After Taylour, 1972)

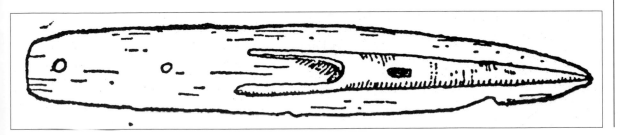

The 'Sea Battle' fresco from Akrotiri on the Aegean island of Thera, 1500 BC. This is one of the very few surviving depictions of an actual formation of Mycenaean heavy infantry. Each of the tower shields is covered with a different coloured or patterned hide, represented in black, brown, grey and yellow. (Courtesy Prehistoric Museum of Thera)

etc. However, he paid for this protection with a serious restriction of his mobility. One could imagine that if a warrior tried to run with such a shield while still holding his spear with both hands, the former would bounce around very awkwardly, banging against his arm, lower face and, particularly, his shins. It is impossible to know when the tower shield was first introduced into the Aegean; no archaeological remains of such shields have been found (doubtless due to the fact that they were made of perishable materials), but the earliest depictions of them occur at Mycenae and are dated to around 1600 BC.

A boss is a common feature of a heavy infantryman's shield throughout the ancient period; it allows the shield to be used offensively. This feature, along with the curve of the surface, would have made the figure-of-eight shield especially good for prising apart enemy shield-walls and breaking into a densely packed formation. In this respect it would have been far superior to the tower shield. The figure-of-eight shield is more technically developed than the tower shield, and is therefore likely to be a somewhat later innovation. As far as is known, the earliest pictures of these shields date from around 1600–1550 BC at Mycenae, but they are found in the same context as the tower shields. The figure-of-eight shield is not flat in profile as some tower shields appear to be, but is concave; it would thereby afford a deflective ability that would greatly increase its strength. In addition it had an elongated 'boss', in the form of a raised ridge of wood or tough leather. This and the characteristic 'waisted' shape, were deliberate elements which must have been developed for practical reasons.

The function of the waist cut-outs is something of a mystery, as there are no actual depictions showing them being put to any direct use. If a line of soldiers formed up in close order with figure-of-eight shields, the cut-outs would form a series of roughly diamond-shaped holes. It is possible that these were useful when the heavy spearman used his secondary weapon, the thrusting sword. Each soldier would have one of these holes to his right front, and could thrust at his enemy through it while still retaining the full-body protection of his shield. This possibility is further supported by the fact that the Mycenaean sword in use at this time was indeed better suited to thrusting than slashing.

It is also conceivable that the series of holes presented in the shield-wall might have accommodated the spear, but this seems unlikely for two related reasons. Firstly, the depictions do not show the spear being used this way; they show it being wielded with both hands, normally at shoulder level and with the shield worn around the back. Secondly, the spears used by these troops would have been both heavy and unwieldy for the warrior to grip in his right hand alone, as he would have to if he were using it to thrust through the shield cut-out; and if he held it near its central point of balance he would both waste half of its length, and disrupt the ranks behind him.

A question remains as to how the figure-of-eight shield was distributed amongst the heavy infantry. It appears to have been used at the same time as the tower shield, but it is unclear whether it was reserved for separate units, or mixed in with tower shields to give the formation a 'biting edge'. Perhaps personal preference or wealth cannot be ruled out.

Spears

The early Mycenaean spear consisted of a long wooden shaft about 12ft long with a socketed spearhead made of bronze. The earliest style of spearhead was of unusual form and is sparsely represented: the blade had a shoe-socket cast on one or both sides of it, into which the split end of the wooden shaft was inserted. Examples have been found at Sesklo, Leukas, Asine and Mycenae, and this style of spearhead seems to be of mainland origin. However, the more common type of spearhead, in use throughout the whole of the Mycenaean period, was a narrow leaf-shaped blade with a strong mid-rib and a socketed base. This was secured to the shaft by a metal collar at the base of the socket, as well as by holes through the socket for pins. The origin of this type seems to be Cretan. Several long, heavy spears of this kind were buried in the Shaft Graves at Mycenae, and depictions show it in use by heavy infantry. Most of the spearheads found date to the early Mycenaean period; not many examples have survived from the

later period, although it continues to appear on later depictions. The reason for this could be the lack of rich graves from the later period.

There were two ways in which the socketed spearhead could be made. They could either be cast with the socket complete, or more simply made with the socket slit and flat; this was then curved around to form a socket, with the slit running laterally along the socket where the two ends were joined. The length of the spearheads from tip to base of socket normally ranged between 8in and 12in, although some are more than 16in long.

Some early depictions show the spear being wielded at the level of the shoulders with both hands, while others seem to be held in the right hand only. However, the method of holding the spear with both hands, horizontal at the level of the shoulder, is only seen when the shield is slung around to the spearman's back. When the warrior is wielding the spear in any other way, he is shown with the shield worn in front of his body.

The boar's-tusk helmet

This type of warrior did not need to wear body armour because of the full-body protection afforded by the large shield. However, it was normal for them to wear a boar's-tusk helmet, for the obvious reason that the head was not protected by the shield. A series of boar's tusks, neatly cut lengthways into oblong plates and pierced in the corners with holes, were sewn on to a conical frame of leather. The direction of the curve of the tusks was made to alternate in each successive row, of which there were normally four or five. The crown of the helmet was either adorned with a plume or terminated in a knob; and some had neck and/or cheek guards. Nearly every representation of a Mycenaean heavy infantryman wears a boar's-tusk helmet. These helmets – a purely Aegean contribution to the history of armour – would not only have looked impressive but would also have been very protective.

13th century BC ivory inlay depicting a warrior wearing a boar's-tusk helmet, from Mycenae. This was probably one of many used to decorate a chest or piece of furniture. Note the cheek guards found on some examples. (Courtesy National Archaeological Museum, Athens)

An image of a boar's-tusk helmet engraved on to a Cretan double axe. (Courtesy Professor Dr H-G.Buchholz)

This type of helmet is fully described by Homer, although it had gone out of use long before his day and did not survive the Mycenaean period. It may have originated in Crete, but it is impossible to know for sure due to a lack of reliably dated finds. One bronze double axehead, said to come from Knossos, has a boar's-tusk helmet engraved on both sides. This axe is dated to between 1700 and 1450 BC; if it does indeed date back to 1700, then it is the oldest known depiction of such a helmet, and suggests that they did originate on Crete. Whatever the case, the mainland adopted it not long after this; an actual example was found at Mycenae, dated to soon after 1550 BC. There are many depictions of the boar's-tusk helmet in Mycenaean art: it is worn by warriors depicted on rings and engravings, it is a popular motif in ivory inlay work, and it is figured on the 'Siege Rhyton' cup fragments. This type of helmet's most popular period appears to have been c.1550–1500 BC, and numerous fragments of the cut and pierced tusks have been found in tombs all over Greece.

Selection of Late Minoan and Mycenaean helmet types taken from depictions and surviving examples. Following the discovery of a suit of bronze armour at Dendra, 'helmet B' has actually been identified as a shoulder piece from such a suit... Due to the abstract nature of depictions such as 'F' and 'H', details of their construction are unknown. (After Ventris & Chadwick)

A   B   C   D

E   F   G   H

Conical bronze helmet with cheek guards, found in a warrior's tomb on Crete and reconstructed from more than a hundred fragments. One of the rare surviving examples of Mycenaean helmets other than the boar's-tusk type, it dates to 1450–1425 BC. (Courtesy Professor Dr H-G.Buchholz)

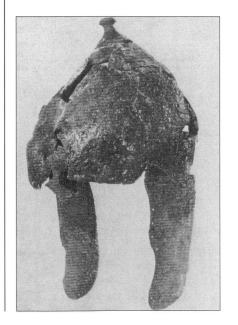

Other helmets

Besides the boar's-tusk helmet, several other types are known. A conical helmet of sheet bronze with cheek pieces was found in one of the Knossian warrior tombs; it is pierced with holes for attaching a felt or leather lining. Dated to about 1450 BC, it therefore probably belongs to the period of Mycenaean control over the region. Other finds of parts of this type of helmet have been made on Rhodes and Cyprus.

Two other types of helmet can be seen on a gold ring and a seal from Grave Circle A at Mycenae, both dated to the 16th century BC. The heavy infantryman on the seal wears an odd type of helmet composed of what look like two thick 'rolls' surmounted by a composite knob and a horn. The helmet worn by a swordsman on the gold ring is of a simple design, possibly made of bronze or thick leather and surmounted by what looks like a tufted cockade or pompon. Another form of helmet is shown on a Creto-Mycenaean vase from a tomb at Isopata, near Knossos. It has six concentric bands which some interpret as strips of leather, and others as thick padding sewn together at intervals. A similar helmet, whose sections have a more pronounced bulge, is shown on the fragments of a faience relief from Mycenae.

Tactical implications

Mycenaean warriors armed with a long spear, a tower or figure-of-eight shield and a helmet fulfilled the typical tactical role of heavy infantrymen. Their weapons and armour tell us this: due to his relative lack of manoeuvrability this type of infantryman needed to be organized in a drilled, close-order formation in order to be effective. A warrior accoutred in this way and fighting on his own would fall easy prey to lighter, more mobile infantry and chariots. Standing alone, his movement is clumsy and slow because he is hampered by his large shield and his long spear; it is easy for a light swordsman, for example, to parry his spear point with one blow from several feet away and then close with him to stab around the clumsy shield before he can draw his own sword to defend himself.

To use some much later analogies that demonstrate similar practical limitations: in the Napoleonic period, when the lance made a resurgence of popularity among light cavalry, it was well known that if a cavalryman armed only with a sabre could get past the lance point, the lancer was done for. Agincourt (1415) provides an even more similar parallel, when the lightly armed, largely unarmoured English archers closed with very heavily armoured dismounted French knights, and exploited their far greater agility to kill them in large numbers with such weapons as daggers and hatchets.

On the other hand, if a heavily equipped warrior is placed shoulder-to-shoulder with several hundred like-armed comrades a very different picture emerges. The large rectangular and figure-of-eight shields held next to each other or even overlapping would present an armoured wall covering the whole battle line from neck to ankle. This would not only render the front ranks almost invulnerable to missiles, but would prevent many missiles from passing into the rear ranks, which smaller shields could not do so effectively. The size of the shields may thus suggest a considerable missile exchange before contact.

In such a massed formation, several ranks deep, the c.12ft spear is far from being impractically long, but is a perfect weapon either for levelling against an opposing line of infantry, or for defence against chariots. In addition, the light troops who would have proved so deadly to an isolated heavy infantryman in the open would themselves be vulnerable if they attempted contact with such a formation.

Swords

Second only in importance to the long, heavy spear in the Mycenaean armoury was the sword or *pakana*, of which abundant examples have been recovered from the Shaft Graves – in which every warrior was apparently equipped with many more than he would have needed during his lifetime. All show noticeably fine workmanship, whether plain, practical examples or richly decorated pieces. The earliest swords (Type A) have rounded shoulders, short tangs and pronounced midribs; the forebears of this type are certainly Minoan. Alongside these thrusting swords (which have been confusingly described as 'rapiers') in the Shaft Graves was found another kind (Type B); these are less well represented than the former, and only one example was found in the earlier Grave Circle B. Sword Type B has square or pointed shoulders, a longer tang and a shorter blade. It may have developed from the flanged

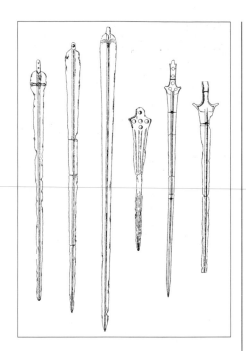

Early Minoan and Mycenaean swords dating from between c.1900 and c.1400 BC. The shorter example, third from right, was actually found in Turkey to where it had been traded. The remainder were discovered in Greece and Crete. (Courtesy Professor Dr H-G.Buchholz)

Minoan and Mycenaean daggers, and sword (second from left). The left-hand dagger is from Crete and is very early, dating to c.2150–1900 BC, long before the appearance of the Mycenaean civilization. The two at right date to the later Mycenaean period, c.1300–1200 BC. (Courtesy Professor Dr H-G.Buchholz)

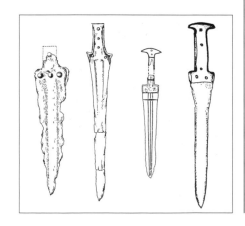

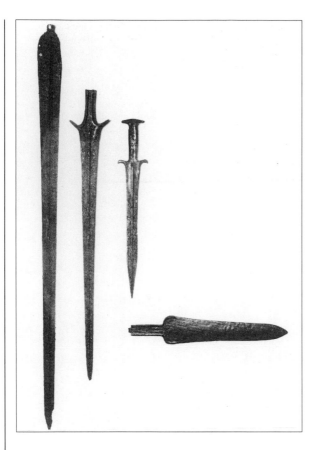

Four excavated swords spanning the Mycenaean period. The left hand example is the early long thrusting sword. The next two date to between c.1400 and c.1200. The short sword at bottom is of the wide-bladed, unfullered, slashing type which was introduced in the later period. (Courtesy National Archaeological Museum, Athens, and Museum of Thebes)

dagger, of which there were several examples in the earlier Grave Circle, but it can also trace its origins to the Near East. A variant of Type B is the horned thrusting sword, the pointed shoulders being extended to form two horns. The cruciform-shouldered rapier also seems to be derived from Type A.

From the beginning of the 14th century BC a new type of sword seems to have been favoured, perhaps due to broadening contacts with the Near East. The old thrusting sword continued in use during the 14th century BC, but was being replaced by a two-edged slashing sword. This new weapon has square shoulders, and these, as well as the hilt, are flanged. The blade is broad, with a widening towards the tip, and has no mid-rib. The earliest examples most probably date to the second half of the 14th century BC. The appearance of these slashing swords is evidence for a change that Mycenaean heavy infantry underwent during the later period, when warriors became lighter and more mobile, suggesting that they fought in more open formations than previously.

Mycenaean infantry carried their swords in a scabbard, sometimes tasselled, worn at the left waist slung from a shoulder belt. This sword served as a secondary weapon for the early heavy infantryman; it would have been useful either if the spear broke, or after the initial push of spear had inevitably developed into a close-quarter mêlée.

Changes from c.1300 BC

In the later Mycenaean period the large body shields and long spears fell out of use. The later Mycenaean spear became much shorter, at around 5–6ft, still tipped with a socketed spearhead. This allowed it to be wielded with one hand, freeing the other for gripping the shield. Some infantry at least (though probably not all) were additionally armed with a sword, carried as before in a leather scabbard worn from a shoulder belt. The later swords were, as described, designed more for slashing than thrusting, being shorter and wider than those of the early period, and with no mid-rib.

Two new patterns of shield were introduced: the round shield or *aspis*, and the 'inverted *pelta*'. As with the earlier types, no remains of these wickerwork and hide shields have survived. Instead of being full-body defences 'worn' by means of the *telamon*, the later shields were carried on the left arm, a development which was carried through to the later hoplite period. Examples of troops carrying the round shield can be found in frescoes from Mycenae, Tiryns and Pylos. It was large enough to cover the torso of the warrior, but also manoeuvrable enough to use in the individual combats that appear to have become more common in the later period. The centre of the shield, being raised, would also have served as a boss, and its curvature would have helped to deflect enemy blows.

The 'inverted *pelta*' pattern was almost round but had a curved cut-out in its lower edge. When carried in front of the body it would protect the warrior's torso, but the cut-out would allow him to run without the lower rim of the shield banging into his upper legs.

With these smaller shields came a need for body armour for the heavy infantry, and corselets were introduced for Mycenaean warriors from c.1200 BC. There are some excellent depictions of troops accoutred in this way on the so-called 'Warrior Vase' and 'Warrior Stele' from Mycenae. These corselets appear to have been made of leather with copper or bronze scales sewn on. The depicted warriors also wear leather skirts that reach to mid-thigh, which could also be reinforced with bronze scales. Although the most notable depictions of this dress come from Mycenae, several other sites show troops similarly equipped, suggesting that its use was widespread.

The later period also saw the introduction of greaves for infantry, metal greaves coming into vogue apparently quite suddenly in around 1200 BC. The adoption of metal greaves was probably linked to the fact that throughout most of the Mycenaean period men protected their legs with leather 'spats' when at work in the fields. The bronze greaves cannot have been very effective since they were relatively thin, one extant pair being only 2mm thick; modern experiments have shown that even a thickness of 3mm can be cut through entirely with a slashing sword. After the middle of the 12th century BC greaves disappear from the archaeological record, so it seems that their use in the early part of that century was a short-lived experiment.

The characteristically Mycenaean boar's-tusk helmet remained popular in the later period, but new patterns were also introduced. These are known as the 'horned helmet' and the 'hedgehog helmet', both terms being derived from the helmets' depicted appearance. As we have no surviving examples of these helmets the details of their construction are unclear. It is likely, however, that they were formed from hard leather. Both the 'horned' and the 'hedgehog' helmet are worn by the otherwise identically dressed warriors portrayed on the so-called 'Warrior Vase' from Mycenae, which is dated to about 1200 BC.

'The Warrior Vase': one of the most detailed depictions of late Mycenaean soldiery, this vase shows two units of spearmen heading out on campaign. The warriors on the side shown here wear 'horned helmets', and on the reverse is a similarly equipped line of warriors wearing 'hedgehog helmets'. (Courtesy National Archaeological Museum, Athens)

The 'horned' helmet has projections at front and rear which come down to protect the brow and the nape of the neck, and another is drawn down to protect the temple. There is also a curious projection on top of the helmet, similar in profile to an axehead, to which a flowing plume is affixed. The helmet takes its name from the fact that two thin, curved horns are shown attached to the front. Whether or not the 'hedgehog' helmet was actually covered with the spined skin of the animal is impossible to know, but there is no real reason to dismiss the idea. The depictions of it on the Warrior Vase show it as being of simple conical shape and covered with short spikes.

It is only from the later period that evidence is found for the Mycenaean warrior using footwear. The soldiers depicted on the Warrior Vase have cross-hatching on their feet, suggesting that they are wearing sandals. This is supported by the discovery at Mallia of a model of a sandalled foot.

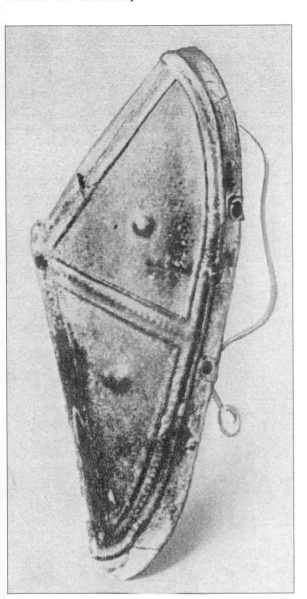

One of a pair of bronze greaves found in a tomb in Achaea. It has holes around the edges through which bronze wires were threaded for attachment. It dates to the end of the Mycenaean period, during the 12th century BC. (Courtesy Professor Dr H-G.Buchholz)

SKIRMISHERS & LIGHT INFANTRY

There are about as many depictions of lighter types of infantry from the early period as there are of heavy infantry. This suggests that light infantry played a significant role in Mycenaean warfare. In all except one early example where light troops appear, heavy infantrymen are also associated with the scene, suggesting that the two troop types were mutually supporting one another in a tactical context.

The lightest warriors of which we know appear on the 'Siege Rhyton' from Grave Circle A at Mycenae, which dates from the second half of the 16th century BC. These warriors are interpreted as being the lightest troop type available to the Mycenaeans because they are actually naked. They have no defensive armour and no headdress, and carry nothing but their weapons. Two weapons are shown, the sling and the bow; since both are missile weapons and the warriors carry no sidearms or even clubs, this strongly suggests that this type of fighting men were not intended to enter into hand-to-hand combat – that they were, in fact, skirmishers.

They are depicted fighting in a loose formation characteristic of skirmish infantry. An archer can be seen between a pair of slingers, and two more behind them, suggesting that these troops were not divided into separate units based on their armament but that all-purpose skirmishers were grouped together. The fact that they are fighting in a loose formation is reinforced by the inclusion in the scene of two heavy infantrymen, with tower shields and long spears, standing in what cannot be interpreted as anything other than a 'shoulder-to-shoulder' formation. Where these heavy spearmen

stand in relation to the swarm of skirmishers is also significant: they are drawn up behind them. This fits with the normal tactical role of skirmishers, which is to cover the front of the main battle line and harass the opposing battle line with missiles, in order to break up or disorder the opposing formation prior to contact with the 'friendly' heavy infantry. This tactic was routine in later ancient warfare, but this depiction shows that it was also known and employed in the Aegean as early as the 16th century BC.

There is also a figure of what is probably a skirmisher on an inlaid dagger from Mycenae. He wears the typical loincloth or short kilt also worn by his heavily armed comrades. His only weapon is a short bow, very similar to those carried by the skirmishers on the Siege Rhyton, and his pose is also very similar to those warriors. As in the Siege Rhyton scene, 'friendly' heavy infantrymen are associated with the archer. In the inlaid dagger scene the archer is the third figure back from the 'enemy' (who is depicted as a lion). The warriors in front of him are heavy infantrymen, of whom there is another behind the archer. The archer is therefore supporting the heavy infantry, as on the Siege Rhyton. The fact that this figure wears the same clothing as the heavy infantry might suggest that he is more of a 'regular' than the naked skirmishers of the Siege Rhyton.

These simple greaves found at Dendra date to the early 14th century BC, which makes them later than the suit of armour found at the same site. They are constructed of very thin bronze plate. (After Astrom)

'The Siege Rhyton' – a drawing of the surviving fragments of the cup. On the relatively large fragment (right) can be seen naked bowmen and slingers skirmishing, as well as a 'unit' of two infantrymen with tower shields. From the city walls people appear to be throwing missiles at the enemy. (After S.Chapman)

Archers

From the Mycenaean period three main types of bow are known: a simple wooden 'self' bow made of a single stave of wood; a sinew-backed bow, i.e. reinforced with sinew glued to the back to prevent breakage and to increase the bow's cast; and a composite bow, which combines layers of horn, wood and sinew to create a weapon with a balance of

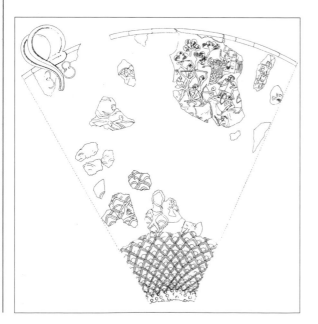

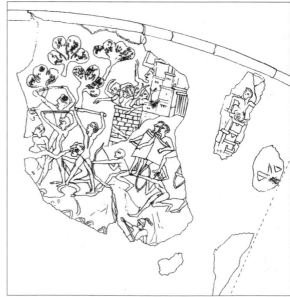

strength under tensile and compressive forces which provides a highly efficient transfer of the energy stored in the fully drawn bow.

The wooden self bow is the simplest and oldest form. Since the earliest direct evidence for wooden bows and arrow shafts dates to the late Upper Palaeolithic period (before c.10,550 BC) in Europe, and possibly to the Upper Palaeolithic and Natufian periods (c.10,550–8,050 BC) in the Levant, we can be sure that they were also the first type used in the Aegean, and probably came into use there at about the same time.

The short wooden bow is difficult to shoot well, since small variations in draw length lead to a great variation in arrow flight and velocity. A wooden longbow, measuring 6ft or more, shoots better and more evenly, but because of its length imposes a relative lack of manoeuvrability on the archer. It is therefore no accident that the appearance of a more accurate, reliable and manoeuvrable type – the composite bow – can be clearly documented soon after the introduction of equid-drawn carts in Mesopotamian warfare in the mid 3rd millennium BC, and following the appearance of horse-drawn chariots in Egypt and the Levant a thousand years later. It is worth noting here that the single depiction we have in Mycenaean art of an archer/chariot combination is dated to this very period (i.e. 16th century BC), and comes from an elite grave at Mycenae. This may tell us two things.

Firstly, assuming that the Mycenaeans actually used this combination, even if only for hunting, it shows that they were familiar with the latest technological innovations which were occurring in the contemporary cultures of Egypt and the Levant. Although the Mycenaean depiction shows the bow-armed chariot in a stag hunt, at this time it was already being used *en masse* in warfare by the Egyptians and Hyksos.

This 16th century BC gold signet ring bears the only known depiction of a Mycenaean bow-armed charioteer. This is a hunting scene, however, and as such should not be regarded as evidence that this combination was used in Mycenaean warfare. (Courtesy National Archaeological Museum, Athens)

Examples of early Mycenaean flint and obsidian arrowheads, of tanged and recessed forms, from various sites in Mycenaean Greece, and dating from between 2150 and 1500 BC. Such arrowheads continued to be used by even wealthy warriors when bronze had come into common use. Note the very skilled workmanship and artistic forms of many in the lower rows. (Courtesy Professor Dr H-G.Buchholz)

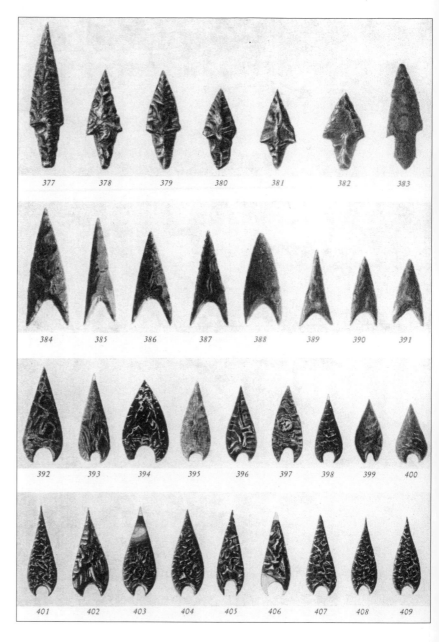

Secondly, since the bow-armed chariot was historically contemporaneous with the composite bow, for reasons noted above, it suggests that the Mycenaean chariot bowman was armed with a composite bow. (This also shows how quick they were to adopt the latest weapons.) The composite bow, when fully drawn, takes a semi-circular curve throughout its length. Allowing for the simplicity of this depiction, the bow shown on it is only half drawn, but looks as if it would become semi-circular when fully drawn, further increasing the likelihood that it is supposed to be a composite bow. The large grip visible on this depiction is also a feature characteristic of composite bows and not found on plain wooden stave bows.

The Siege Rhyton from Mycenae also shows bowmen. It is more difficult to suggest the type of bow these warriors are using, due to the very simplistic treatment. The clearest one is long enough to be a single-stave longbow. The fact that the bowmen are naked and in loose formation suggests that they are poor irregular troops who would presumably arm themselves with the cheapest type of weapon, the self bow.

The archer portrayed on an inlaid dagger from the same grave as the above two artefacts is relatively detailed and less abstracted than the other depictions, but determining the type of bow shown is still difficult. What is immediately noticeable is that it is quite small, which in itself is an indication that it is supposed to be a composite bow. The curve of the bow, although only half drawn, also looks like that of a composite bow, making this the most likely type. This suggests that the more 'regular' skirmisher bowmen such as this one might have been better armed with composite bows than their poorer, irregular comrades; it is even possible that these bows were issued by the palace military organization.

Turning to the arrows themselves, there is ample evidence in the form of substantial finds of arrowheads in several Mycenaean sites. Although bronze arrowheads became widespread with the development of bronze-working technology, flint and obsidian arrowheads – presumably relatively cheaper and more expendable – continued to be used alongside bronze down to about 1400 BC.

Unfortunately, arrowheads cannot be used to form a chronological typology on the basis of their forms, in the way that pottery, for example, often can. Historical and ethnographic evidence has shown that it was usual for military archers to carry several different types of arrows in their quivers at once, so that they could use heavy arrows at short range to pierce armour, or lighter arrows to harass an enemy at long range.

Development of Aegean arrowheads, diagram of types:
EH/EM = 2500–2150 BC
MH/MM = 2150–1550 BC
LH/LM I = 1550–1500 BC
LH/LM II = 1500–1400 BC
LH/LM III A = 1400–1300 BC
LH/LM III B = 1300–1200 BC
LH/LM III C = 1200–1100 BC
(Courtesy Professor Dr H-G.Buchholz)

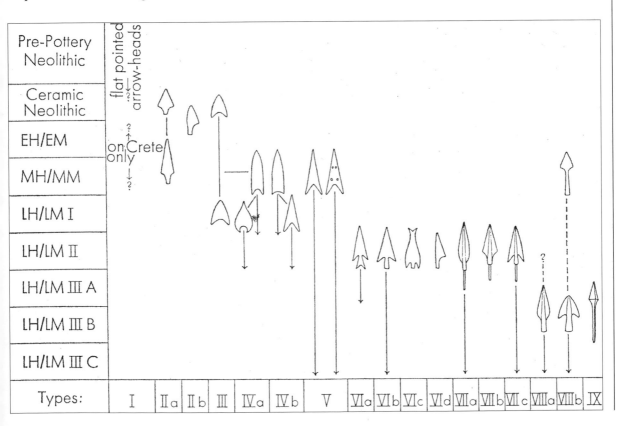

Tanged projectile points. These were simply cut from bronze plate, and thus would have been economical to produce in large numbers. The two largest points may be light javelin heads.
(© The Trustees of the British Museum)

Because flint continued to be used for arrowheads even when the use of bronze was widespread, it is also unconvincing to create a chronology on the basis of what arrows were made of. The only remaining means of determining the relative age of arrowheads is through stratigraphic dating (i.e. the soil level in which the artefact was found), and such records are often incomplete. Attempts to distinguish between arrowheads and points assumed to be javelin heads found in the same assemblage, solely on the basis of arbitrary size and weight limits, must also be avoided in the absence of supporting evidence.

Whether made from bronze or stone, there are three basic methods by which Aegean arrowheads were fixed to the shafts: by means of a tang, a recessed base or a socket. Naturally, socketed arrowheads are only made from metal, since the socketing of heads was made possible by advances in metal casting techniques. Tanged and recessed-based arrowheads are found in both bronze and stone examples. These types of arrowheads seem to have been significantly more numerous than the socketed variety, perhaps for economic reasons. Unlike socketed arrowheads, which had to be cast in special moulds, tanged or recessed-base arrowheads were simply cut out of bronze plate.

One of the earliest types of arrowhead was also the longest-used. These were made from bronze plate, triangular, with a V-shaped recessed base which formed barbs when attached to the shaft. This type was used from c.2000 BC right down to the end of the Mycenaean

The 'Battle in the Glen' ring from Mycenae, 16th century BC. This is an interesting composition, showing two swordsmen in combat while a spearman remains on the defensive behind his tower shield. Note the prominence given to the central swordsman figure. This scene may relate to a long-lost myth or event. (Courtesy National Archaeological Museum, Athens)

period. It is perhaps no coincidence that this was one of the oldest and longest-serving bronze types, since it would have been the easiest to produce in large numbers, and thus the most suitable for large scale issue to soldiers.

It might be logical to suppose that the cast bronze arrowheads which came into use from about 1500 BC onwards would have been employed mainly by the upper classes of warriors. In fact, however, most of the flint and obsidian arrowheads known to us were found in the very rich burials of elite warriors. Stone arrowheads fell out of use after about 1400 BC.

Light infantry swordsmen

In addition to skirmishers, there is also pictorial evidence that the Mycenaeans employed a form of battlefield light infantry. To define our terms, light infantry are a type of troops that fit somewhere between heavy infantry and skirmishers in terms of a balance between mobility, protection and offensive value. They are generally capable of fighting either in massed units or as skirmishers. Light infantry were useful to ancient armies for several reasons. Their flexibility of employment meant that they could fill the tactical gap between (in this case) the massed heavy infantry and the very light skirmishers.

Because light infantry are sometimes required to fight in massed formations, they need to be more capable of sustaining hand-to-hand combat than skirmishers, who are supposed to evade close combat. This hand-to-hand capability, coupled with their ability to operate in loose formations, made light infantry perfect for fighting over broken or mountainous terrain, and one can easily understand why the Greeks would have found such troops useful, given the landscape of the region. Heavy infantry are unsuited to fighting over broken, overgrown or steep ground because of the difficulty of manoeuvring in close order formation in such terrain, and because of the non-linear nature of combat imposed by such an environment. Very light skirmishers are sufficiently manoeuvrable to deploy in such conditions with ease, but because of their lack of mêlée weapons and armour are unsuitable if it is desired to close with the enemy.

25

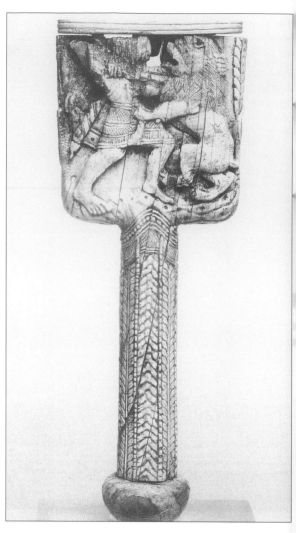

ABOVE **This fine ivory mirror handle from Cyprus is interesting because it portrays a common Mycenaean motif, that of a swordsman slaying a lion. Dating to around the 13th century BC, this depiction shows that the appearance of Mycenaean swordsmen did not alter much throughout the period. (Courtesy Director of Department of Antiquities, Cyprus)**

ABOVE LEFT **Later Mycenaean daggers, dated to between 1400 and 1100 BC. Later weapons such as these are characterized by their one-piece construction and wide blades. They would originally have had inlaid grips of wood or bone. (Courtesy Professor H-G.Buchholz)**

The earliest pictorial evidence for Mycenaean use of light infantry comes from the 16th century BC Shaft Graves at Mycenae. This is in the form of a cylinder seal and a ring, of which both seem to show a similar type of light infantry swordsman. Turning first to the cylinder seal, the scene depicts a warrior wearing the characteristic kilt and armed with a long, straight sword, stabbing a heavy infantryman in the throat over the top rim of the latter's figure-of-eight shield. This scene vividly depicts the reason that light infantry could be useful against heavy infantry: the swordsman has managed to get past the heavy infantryman's spear point, leaving the latter at the mercy of his more agile opponent. This swordsman is obviously 'lighter' than his adversary, because he does not carry a shield. He cannot be a skirmisher, because he does not have a missile weapon and is engaged in close combat with a heavy infantryman. The fact that a light infantryman was given such prominence in art as to be shown slaying a heavy spearman suggests that light infantry were respected in Mycenaean warfare; on this seal the light swordsman is clearly the 'hero' of the scene. Historically, more often than not, the lighter the troop type, the poorer and less respected they were; and apart from their lowly social status, skirmishers who did not close with the enemy were sometimes regarded as using cowardly or 'dirty' tactics – that was how Classical Greek hoplites saw light troops.

The fresco fragment from Mycenaean Knossos, 1450–1400 BC, named 'The Captain of the Blacks' a century ago. This shows what appears to be a Greek javelinman leading a unit of African mercenaries; the main figure's skin colour is brown, that of the other figure, black. The yellow/orange 'kilt' has a black and white border. (Courtesy Ashmolean Museum)

Fresco from Pylos, 13th century BC, depicting a skirmish between Mycenaean light infantry and 'barbarians'. This shows the Pylian light infantrymen in very uniform dress. The straps across their chests are for the sword scabbard, and note that one carries a spear. The 'kilts' have a black overlay, probably of leather. See Plate F. (Courtesy Department of Classics, University of Cincinnati)

The evidence from the Mycenaean world, however, contradicts this attitude; it even seems that light swordsmen actually enjoyed higher status than the spearmen of the line, being regarded as 'champions' (*promachoi*). In Mycenaean depictions light infantry are portrayed with respect for their bravery, and given a prominence that suggests that they were an integral part of the army as a whole.

Another and similar depiction of this type of light infantryman can be seen on the so-called 'Battle in the Glen' ring. Like the previous example, it comes from a Shaft Grave at Mycenae and is dated to the second half of the 16th century BC. Here too a swordsman is depicted in a heroic light. The scene shows, on the left, a fallen man – no weapon or armour is visible, but he is probably a warrior. A central figure is armed with what appears to be a short sword or long dagger, and wears a kilt and a boar's-tusk helmet. This warrior is about to stab another swordsman, who is kneeling and trying to stab his attacker with a long straight sword; this man also wears a helmet, though it does not appear to be of the boar's-tusk type. At far right is a heavy infantryman with a tower shield, long spear and boar's-tusk helmet, adopting a defensive posture. This scene is interesting in that it shows two light infantrymen in combat against one another with the heavy infantryman more or less on the sidelines.

Due to the specific subject matter of this scene, it probably depicts a long-lost story or myth; however, it is still a very useful depiction of Mycenaean light infantry. It shows that they could wear helmets, and if some really did wear the boar's-tusk type it reinforces the idea that these troops had a relatively high status. That they wear helmets but do not carry shields is in keeping with the needs of the light infantryman to have some protection while needing to remain lightly equipped and mobile. The presence of a heavy infantryman in the scene further supports the likelihood that light infantry worked in support of and in conjunction with heavy infantry. It also shows that light infantry sometimes confronted each other, which is understandable if both sides were using the same tactical doctrine.

The weapons shown in the hands of these warriors are also characteristically Mycenaean, i.e. the long, straight stabbing sword and the sturdy dagger or short sword. It may even be possible to identify the sword types used in these depictions from actual examples. For example, the long, straight sword held by the kneeling warrior in the Battle in the Glen ring could be the so-called Sandars Type A, one of which was actually found in the same grave circle as the ring, and is of contemporary date. The sword being wielded by the swordsman on the cylinder seal from the Shaft Grave has a very distinctively shaped hilt, which looks very close to that of the Sandars Type CII sword. However, this presents a chronological problem: the CII sword is dated to around 1400 BC, whereas the seal is from the second half of the 16th century BC. Perhaps this seal is evidence that this pattern of sword was introduced much earlier than was previously thought. The type of short, wide-bladed dagger with which the other swordsman on the Battle in the Glen ring is armed was a common Mycenaean weapon, as attested by numerous finds in the Aegean region.

A third possible example of this type of warrior is depicted on another 16th century cylinder seal from Mycenae, although – since he is depicted fighting a lion – he is strictly speaking a hunter rather than a warrior. However, he is armed and dressed exactly the same as the parallel examples discussed above. He is not wearing a helmet. Like the ring discussed above, this scene probably relates to a story or myth, and this idea is supported by the depiction of a very similar scene on an ivory mirror handle from around 1200 BC. The similarity of the pose of both man and lion in both depictions, though four centuries apart, is striking. Alternatively, the lion may be a symbol of 'the enemy'.

Tactical implications

The most likely tactical use of such swordsmen as depicted on the Shaft Grave goods was as a kind of light infantry which fought against, and in conjunction with, the heavy infantry. They seem to have held a relatively high status, partly because they went into battle without shields and took on heavy infantry (and, most likely, chariots too). They would have been most effective if gathered in fairly large units in a loose, yet organized formation. Not being 'screening' troops like skirmishers, they would need to be in massed units in order to have enough solidity and impetus to engage effectively in mêlées with heavier infantry. They would have been extremely effective against disordered heavy infantry, breaking into the latter's formation and cutting it apart. If heavy infantry were fleeing, a timely rush by a fresh unit of light swordsmen would be able to outrun them with lethal results. Another likely deployment might have been to guard the flanks of the main heavy infantry battle line from enemy attacks – one of the main historical roles of light infantry, both in Greece and elsewhere, since a closely ordered battle line of heavy infantry is inherently vulnerable to flank attack. In summation, these swordsmen would have played an important role in Mycenaean warfare, which may also explain their prominence in the artistic record.

Javelinmen

Besides swordsmen, the so-called 'Captain of the Blacks' fresco from Mycenaean Knossos shows another type of light infantry – javelinmen. The fresco fragment shows a running man in the usual male flesh colour of reddish-brown, but also the upper leg of another man with black skin, as well as a fragment of the latter's head. Sir Arthur Evans, excavator of Knossos, saw the brown (i.e. Greek) warrior as the officer of what he believed to have been a line of African mercenaries, hence the name given to the fresco.

It was common in ancient warfare for javelinmen to carry two light javelins (Mycenaean, *pataja*). The main figure on the fresco carries just such a pair of light javelins and this, coupled with his lack of any armour, identifies him as a light infantryman. Being so armed he could technically be a skirmisher; but the appearance of the black-skinned man's leg close behind him, wearing a similar kilt and in the same pose, suggests that the two are part of a unit and in an ordered formation. The black warrior shown on the fresco fragment is generally called a Nubian mercenary. Apart from the skin colour, the other reason for this is the two feathers which can be seen in the hair of both the Greek and the African behind him. Some have interpreted the warriors as wearing a 'bristly hat' with horns, but this looks rather more like the warrior's hair; ancient depictions of Nubians do not show them wearing horned hats, but either leather caps or headbands with one or two standing feathers. Nubians were renowned as good light troops and were employed as mercenaries by the Egyptians. The most likely interpretation of the fresco is therefore that it shows a unit of Nubian javelinmen, wearing native headdress along with a Mycenaean kilt. They are led by a Greek officer, who wears the Nubian feathers as a badge of his unit and to identify him as their officer.

There is also another obscure fresco fragment from Mycenaean Knossos (called by Evans 'Warriors Hurling Javelins'), showing what are probably javelin-armed light infantry. There are several similarities between this and the fresco discussed above, which indicate that javelin-armed light infantry were an actual troop type. The two frescoes are painted quite differently, showing that they do not come from the same scene. Some of the warriors in the Warriors Hurling Javelins fresco are wearing white 'necklaces' of the same type as the Captain of the Blacks, and all are wearing the same kilt. They are portrayed in a rather densely packed unit, hurling javelins upwards at about a 45-degree angle, possibly at an enemy battlement or perhaps over the heads of other infantry. There is also what can only be an officer standing with a long staff or javelin. All this suggests that they are light infantry of the same Mycenaean troop type as the supposed Nubians; however, they are not Africans but a Greek unit.

Changes from c.1300 BC

Depictions from the later Mycenaean period are conspicuous for the predominance of lighter equipped warriors. Unlike the heavy infantry, later Mycenaean light infantry did not undergo any radical transformations in their equipment or tactical doctrine. The short explanation for this is that they did not need to: it was the cumbersome heavy infantry that needed to become more mobile to confront changing enemy tactics, not the already well-developed light infantry. However, there are some notable changes in their dress and equipment that first appear during this later period.

Many Mycenaean light infantrymen in this period wore a tunic, probably of linen. This garment was short-sleeved, cut to taper in around the waist and then flare out again, and extended to just above the knee. Another garment worn by the light infantry of the palace of Pylos was a white cloth kilt, with a protective leather overlay cut so that its ends formed pointed tassels hanging down. Later Mycenaean light troops also commonly wore linen greaves, tied at the ankle and

Gravestone from a 16th century BC shaft grave in the Mycenaean citadel. This is one of the earliest depictions of the chariot in Mycenaean art, and shows a box chariot riding down an enemy swordsman. (Courtesy National Archaeological Museum, Athens)

below the knee and reinforced over the shins. The boar's-tusk helmet remained popular; a fresco from Pylos depicting light infantrymen armed with spear and sword fighting 'barbarians' shows the troops all wearing the same pattern of boar's-tusk helmet.

Depictions of later light infantry show them armed with a sword, and a short spear or javelin. The swordsmen continued to carry their weapon in a scabbard worn from a shoulder belt. Although there are no depictions of later archers, their existence is attested by the discovery of many mass-produced arrowheads at Pylos. Likewise there is no pictorial evidence (or archaeological, for that matter) for slingers in the later Mycenaean army. However, an explanation for this may be that slingers were recruited from the civilian population when the need arose and supplied their own weapon, as in the early period.

CHARIOTRY

The Greeks were quick to adopt the chariot for use in warfare. In the 16th century BC, over little more than a hundred years, the spoked-wheel war chariot became familiar in an area extending from Greece to India, and from south Russia to Egypt. The apparent abruptness of this widespread appearance, and the close similarity in form between chariots over the whole area at the beginning of the Late Bronze Age, has long encouraged the view that their spread must be attributed to a specific people. In fact, this was the second, not the first stage in a process of innovation and diffusion in which many factors are still obscure.

What we do know is that the fully developed war chariot is shown on several late 16th century BC gravestones from Mycenae, as well as on a ring found in one of the Shaft Graves. This is roughly the same time that it appeared in Egypt. Although most probably diffused from the Near East after the Middle Bronze Age (c.1950–1550 BC), as a result of Mycenae's likely trade contacts with that region, no single ethnic or linguistic group seems to have been the master innovator in the history of horse-drawn chariotry in the Near East. Interestingly, unlike most Mycenaean military technology, the chariot does not seem to have come to the mainland via Crete, but the other way around; it was not until the mid-15th century BC that it appears on that island, listed on the Mycenaean Linear B tablets.

The Aegean chariot

Whenever possible, the battleground chosen by Mycenaean armies was a relatively level and open area on which opposing forces could array themselves. Due to the set-piece, linear nature of ancient warfare there was no question of an extended front over unprepared ground. The reason for this was simply that if one side offered battle on terrain which would seriously hamper the adversary's ability to use his troops effectively, the adversary would refuse battle.

Despite the apparently brutal simplicity of such confrontations, they did involve quite complex calculations which took into account various factors such as time restrictions, the ultimate objectives of the particular campaign, lines of communication, and even weather. The basic goal was to force the enemy into battle on terrain that was disadvantageous to them. The fact that battles were fought on chosen ground rather than

(Continued on page 41)

EARLY INFANTRY, c.1500 BC
1: Theran heavy spearman
2: Swordsman
3: Heavy spearman

A

EARLY INFANTRY, 16th–15th CENTURIES BC
1: Light infantry swordsman, 16th century BC
2: Creto-Mycenaean javelinman, c.1450 BC
3: Heavy spearman, 16th century BC

B

EARLY MISSILE TROOPS, 16th–15th CENTURIES BC
1: Regular archer, 16th century BC
2: Irregular slinger, 16th century BC
3: Nubian mercenary javelinman, 1450–1400 BC

D

DUAL CHARIOT, 1500–1400 BC
1: Warrior in corselet, c.1400 BC
2: Charioteer, 15th century BC
3: Swordsman, 15th century BC

LATER INFANTRY, c.1250–1200 BC
1 & 2: Mycenaean spearmen
3: Pylian infantryman

E

PYLIAN LIGHT INFANTRY & 'BARBARIANS',
   c.1250–1200 BC
1: Light spearman
2: Swordsman
3: Barbarian

F

RAIL CHARIOT, c.1250–1150 BC
1: Charioteer
2: Spearman

1: Mounted warrior, c.1200 BC
2: Mycenaean woman

H

randomly is important to the understanding of the use of the chariot in Mycenaean warfare. Although no one can credibly argue that chariots were not used *en masse* in the contemporary armies of the Near East, many have argued that they could not have been used in a similar way in Greece, on the grounds that Greece's terrain is too mountainous to accommodate tactics developed on the broad, flat plains of the Near East. This argument is unconvincing for several reasons.

It is true that chariots only work effectively on relatively open ground; but a study of the topography surrounding important Mycenaean and Minoan centres shows that they all border plains. Mycenae and Tiryns have the Argive Plain, Pylos the Messenian Plain, Phaestos the Plain of Messara, and so forth. These level areas did not have to be as large as those of the Near East to be suitable battlegrounds, because the armies involved would only have taken up a relatively limited amount of space. While the Mycenaeans had immediate access to amply-sized plains just outside the gates of their citadels, the fact remains that these plains were still generally rougher, rockier and more broken than those of the Near East. However, the Mycenaeans evidently did not let this stop them from using massed chariots; they simply made their chariots heavier and more robust than their light Egyptian and Near Eastern contemporaries. The Aegean chariot, from its earliest depictions at Mycenae in the 16th century BC and throughout the Mycenaean period, kept the four-spoked wheels seen on other chariots, but made them stronger and more robust, a characteristic visible when compared with, for instance, Egyptian chariots. The draught pole was strengthened by a wooden support with

13th century BC fresco from Pylos showing a dual chariot in use in the later period. Although of an old type, this example appears more lightly constructed than early dual chariots; perhaps it was now used more for transporting infantry than charging – the spearman marching behind the chariot is the kind of warrior who would ride in it. Note the waisted tunics characteristic of depictions of later-period troops; and the boar's-tusk helmets, both with neck guards, one with a knob at the apex and one with a curved tusk. (Courtesy Department of Classics, University of Cincinnati)

Fragments of a ceramic vessel from Tiryns, late 12th century BC, apparently showing rail chariots. In the chariot to the right, part of an infantryman with a round shield and spear can be seen riding with the driver. These were the last type of Mycenaean chariot to be used and were of the lightest construction. (Courtesy Nauplia Museum)

cross-bracing. It is possible than this characteristically Aegean second shaft extended backwards as an integral part of the structure of the cab. If these chariots had only been employed to drive the elite along the Mycenaean road system, there would have been no need for such strengthening.

Throughout the Mycenaean period only the two-horse chariot was used, but various types are distinguishable. The earliest type that appears in the Mycenaean period is termed the box chariot, whose period of use was c.1550–1450 BC. It is so named because the cab was basically box-shaped, having a more or less rectangular profile. Its sides rose up to hip height or somewhat lower and were covered with screening material, possibly wickerwork. Although this type of chariot is of oriental origin, its prototypes appearing on Syrian seals of the 18th–17th centuries BC, it already displays typically Aegean features.

The dual chariot, used c.1450–1200 BC (with possible extensions at either end of that time range), is so named because its cab consisted of two distinct parts: the cab proper, and curved extensions or 'wings' added to the sides at the rear. The floor was D-shaped, probably being made of interwoven leather thongs which would have served as a kind of suspension system for the occupants. The siding extended around the front and sides and rose to approximately hip height. The curved side projections may have more clumsily served the same purpose as the sweeping handrail found on Egyptian chariots. These would have been of great assistance both in mounting the chariot, and as guards from the wheels should the horses at any moment turn or back unexpectedly. In addition they may have acted as 'mudguards' against flying stones and dust. The sides and wings were covered by some sort of screening material such as leather or linen. Documents describe these chariots as being painted various shades of red, some being decorated with ivory inlay.

A rare type of chariot, known only from one or two carved representations, is termed the quadrant chariot; its representations date to c.1450–1375 BC. Unlike other Mycenaean chariots this type is only shown carrying one occupant. This could mean that it was not used in war. It appears to have had a D-shaped floor like the dual chariot. Its siding consisted of what were probably heat-bent rails, the rounded profile approaching the quadrant of a circle. Like the other chariots its sides rose to approximately hip height and were covered with screening.

The last type of Mycenaean chariot to appear was the rail chariot, dated from c.1250 BC down to 1150 BC. Its cab could hold two occupants abreast. This was an extremely light vehicle, its sides comprising an open framework of rails rising to approximately hip height, with a rounded profile.

Chariot armament

We have seen how the form of the Aegean chariot was adapted to the local terrain by making it heavier and more robust. This, and the armament of the charioteers who rode in them, can suggest the most likely tactical use of these chariots in warfare.

There seems to be only one indubitable example of a chariot crewed by an archer in Mycenaean-Minoan representations. This comes in the form of a gold signet ring from Mycenae and is dated to around 1550–1500 BC. All other depictions of chariots in this early period show them carrying warriors armed with a long spear, similar to that carried by the heavy infantry. A carved gem from Vapheio on the southern tip of Greece shows the driver as well as the warrior. It would have been absolutely necessary to have a separate driver for a war chariot, because it would be impossible to control the chariot and wield a weapon at the same time. Therefore, when only the warrior is depicted – as in the example of a sculpted gravestone at Mycenae – it must be assumed that in reality there would have been a driver as well. (This depiction is highly stylized, which might also account for the lack of a depicted driver.)

Although some have argued that the Mycenaean spear-armed chariots were used for display and transport to and from the battleground, the evidence strongly suggests that spears were actually used from the chariot. The gravestone referred to above actually shows the chariot warrior impaling a sword-armed infantryman with his spear. This tells us firstly that the long spear was used from the back of the chariot in close combat, and secondly that chariots could be used in this way against infantry, not just opposing chariots.

Unfortunately, it may never be possible to discern any of the specifics of Mycenaean chariot tactics due to the extreme lack of descriptive evidence. Some basic questions can nevertheless be answered directly from the available evidence, and others are implied by such evidence as the relevant Linear B tablets from Knossos.

Turning first to these tablets, the large number of chariots listed (400-plus at any one time) suggests that they were used *en masse*. Such numbers would be much more than those needed only for the transport of nobles, even allowing extra chariots as spares. Furthermore, the chariots in which the nobles/commanders might have ridden actually seem to be listed separately in these tablets, in the form of 33 chariots inlaid with ivory. These inlaid chariots may also have been for purely ceremonial use, but that still leaves at least 367 other chariots assembled at Knossos shortly before its final destruction. While it must be conceded

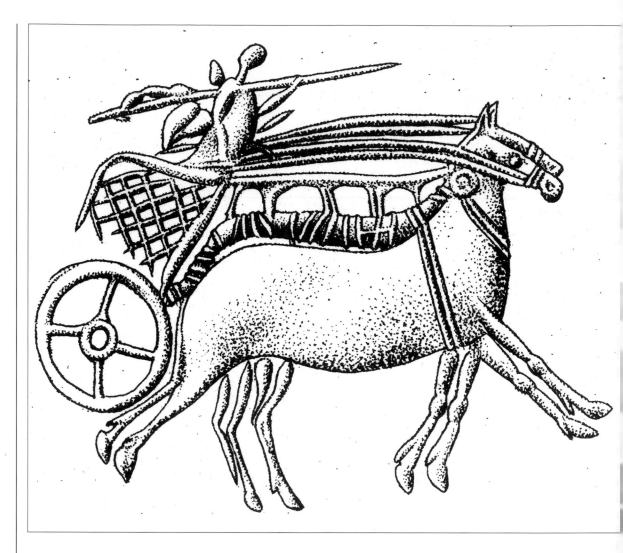

This scene showing an early period Mycenaean box chariot is found engraved on a carnelian seal from Vapheio dated to the 15th century BC. This is one of the few depictions that shows the spearman as well as the driver in the chariot. The sturdy double upper-and-lower draught pole with lashed braces is very prominently shown. (Courtesy National Archaeological Museum, Athens)

that this number of chariots is still immeasurably smaller than the bodies of chariotry deployed by the Egyptians and Hittites on the more open battlefields of Syria, this in itself does not preclude their use as a massed shock force.

Such a force could be used to deliver the *coup de grace* when the enemy was recoiling or about to break, to outflank the enemy battle line, or to pursue a broken enemy force. The use of chariots against disorganized troops is relatively well attested in ancient literature, both the ancient Chinese and the Hittites being aware of their benefits in this role. The roughness of the Greek plains and the limited space for the massed use of chariots may have been an important reason for the relatively small numbers of them fielded (as reflected in the Knossos tablets) compared to the Egyptians or Hittites. This topographical limitation is presumably why they did not form the backbone of the Mycenaean tactical doctrine, as was the case among the Egyptians and Hittites.

Experiments in reconstructing an 18ft-long Macedonian *sarissa* (possibly of similar length to the Mycenaean chariot spear) showed that it had to be held near its centre to stop it overbalancing to the front. This would certainly be a problem if it was held with one hand, but not so if it was held with both hands in a similar manner to that held by heavy infantrymen. The carnelian gem from Vapheio shows a chariot warrior holding the long spear near its rear with both arms partially extended in this manner. On the other hand, the more stylized Mycenaean gravestone shows a spear being held with the right hand only (the left is grasping a sheathed sword). When trying to interpret stylized depictions it is possible to work out the most likely realistic elements, distinguishing those features that would actually work in real life from those that would not. By these criteria, the more realistic pose is that shown on the Vapheio gem rather than that on the grave stele.

In order to use the two-handed spear effectively from the chariot, the Mycenaeans would have had to find a way to deal with the problem that due to the rocking motion of the chariot, and the jolt received when the spear struck home, the warrior who had no hand free to steady himself would lose his balance. Projecting from the underside of some depictions of dual chariots can be seen a small 'spur'; no one is sure what this was or what its function might have been. One possibility is that it is the end of a central rail, a continuation of the pole-stay, which passed through the cab between the two occupants. The warrior could have used this to brace his rear leg when delivering a thrust, thereby preventing his unintentional exit to the rear.

The chariot 'charge'

Early Mycenaean chariots would not have charged at speed at enemy formations in the manner of medieval cavalry. This would have led to them crashing into opposing chariots and infantry with terrible destruction to *both* sides, and would result in the warrior becoming disarmed once he had struck with the spear for the first time. It is more likely that they would have taken the more sensible approach of starting at speed, to minimize the casualties suffered from missiles, and slowing down just before contact with a line of infantry. Even at a trot the impetus of two horses and a chariot bearing down upon foot-soldiers would still be considerable – and especially so if the infantry were disordered. While it is well known that cavalry horses will not willingly run straight into a mass of infantry, the psychological threat posed by a charge has very often proved sufficient to disorder infantry formations just before actual impact. A line of chariots attacking in such a way would be able to achieve the same, especially given the weapons reach afforded to their crews by long spears. The need to defend against this could be one of the reasons that the Mycenaean heavy infantry were equipped and formed in the way they were – with long spear and large shield, in close-order formations. Of course, the chariot teams – like all war horses – would have to be well trained in this form of attack to stop them from swerving or bolting.

Confronting opposing chariotry, the charioteers would probably have tried to avoid crashing into each other, the warriors using their spears to strike at the opposing horses and crews. The fact that the early Mycenaean chariot warriors are not equipped with shields can be recognized as evidence that they fought from their chariots. As with the heavy infantry, the long spears with which the chariot warriors were armed would be an impediment to a foot-soldier unless he also had a

The 15th century BC articulated bronze corselet found at Dendra. This masterpiece of Mycenaean bronze-working is the most complete example found, although there is evidence that such armours were not uncommon in the Mycenaean army. Their use was probably limited to the highest class of chariot-borne warriors. (George Mylonas, *Mycenae and the Mycenaean Age*, © 1966 Princeton University Press; reprinted by permission of Princeton University Press)

large shield and fought in close order with like-armed comrades. If these chariot spearmen had dismounted to fight without shields they would have been nearly useless.

A depiction of an early chariot on a carved gravestone from Mycenae shows both a warrior armed with a long spear and a sheathed sword attached to the outside of the chariot cab, in a manner reminiscent of Egyptian arrow quivers. This is most likely a secondary weapon, logically provided for use if the spear were lost or broken or if the warrior had to abandon the vehicle.

A mid 16th century BC ring from one of the Shaft Graves at Mycenae depicts a chariot crewed by a driver and an archer. This is one of the earliest depictions of a Mycenaean chariot, roughly contemporary with that on the carved gravestone. Unlike the inlaid dagger described earlier, which at face value depicts a hunt but probably had a deeper meaning, this ring does not suggest that it is depicting anything more than a nobleman's hunt. Also unlike the inlaid dagger, the weapon and equipment shown are perfectly suited to hunting, and the emphasis placed on the chariot horses rather than the chariot itself also conveys a non-military feeling.

None of the three chariot-sculpted shaft gravestones show archers; however, this signet ring came from the grave of a man who can have been at no great temporal remove from the introduction of this Asiatic combination of bow and chariot. The fact that this combination was shown contemporary with an indubitable example of a spear-armed chariot warrior in warfare further supports the likelihood that the signet ring's subject matter was intentionally that of the hunt. This being the case, there is no credible evidence for Mycenaean chariots being crewed with bowmen for warfare – a major difference between Mycenaean chariot tactics and those of Egypt, for example.

The Dendra armour

At Dendra, near the Mycenaean citadel of Midea, Greek and Swedish excavations found a chamber tomb which contained a suit of bronze armour which is dated to about 1400 BC. This set of bronze plate defences displays advanced skills in metalworking and armour design. The various pieces, e.g. shoulder guards, skirt, and cuirass, were fitted to one another and attached with leather thongs, allowing the various plates to slide over one another and affording the wearer some limited movement of the body and limbs. The pieces of a boar's-tusk helmet with bronze cheek guards were found with the armour, as were a bronze neck guard which sat atop the shoulders, bronze greaves and arm guards. A knife or dagger with a single cutting edge was also found.

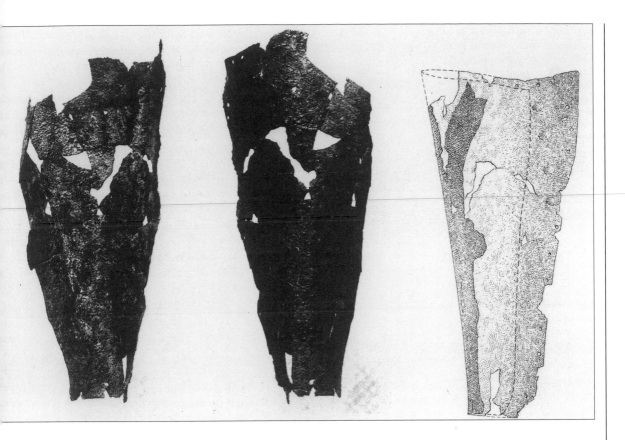

15th century BC bronze forearm guards from Dendra. Defences such as these were probably worn with the bronze corselets. (After Astrom)

There was originally a sword in the tomb, of which only two gilded rivets from the hilt survived; and there may also have been an arrow quiver and a shield, these last two items only surviving as patches of blackish material. (What some have suggested was a shield may instead have been a cover for the large two-handled basin also found in the tomb.)

This is by no means the only example of Late Bronze Age Aegean bronze armour to have been found. Nine other sites have yielded examples of armour made from bronze plate. These include greaves and helmets, as well as pieces which seem to have come from the same type of armour as the Dendra example. Phaistos, Mycenae and another tomb at Dendra have all revealed pieces like this.

This type of armour seems, then, to have been in reasonably widespread use between c.1500 and 1400 BC in the Mycenaean world. The use of plate for armour continued throughout the remainder of the Mycenaean period, but what is significant here is the fact that it was so developed in the early part of the period. This shows that the Dendra panoply was not a 'one-off' created for an innovative warlord who took it to the grave with him. Rather, it seems to have been a relatively well established type of Mycenaean military equipment.

Interestingly, the Linear B tablets from Knossos and Pylos both have ideograms which seem to indicate these armour corselets. The Knossos tablets show the issue of at least 36 corselets, and on nine tablets the corselet has been erased and an ingot inserted instead. This may be intended to be an issue of metal required to make corselets. In the majority of cases the relevant numbers associated with a corselet ideogram have been lost, so it is unknown how many more might have

One of the rare depictions of horse-soldiers in Mycenaean art, from a late period vase fragment. The artist's unfamiliarity with the subject matter may be the reason for the way the 'rider' is shown beside the horse, although he is holding the reins. (Courtesy National Archaeological Museum, Athens)

been listed. The Pylos tablets list 20 corselets; and in addition, the Pylos corselet ideograms have a triangular shape on top of them. This looks like a helmet, and the Pylos tablets actually mention helmets along with the corselets.

A clue as to the use of the Knossos corselets may be found in the fact that each of those tablets is introduced by a man's name, and itemises corselets, wheeled chariots and horses. This strongly suggests that the corselets were worn by at least some chariot-borne warriors. Eight of the tablets list 'one corselet' and 14 list 'two corselets'. This could mean either that some men were issued with two corselets for themselves, or that some men were issued with one corselet for themselves plus one for their driver. Those crews who did not possess a suit of bronze armour (presumably the majority) wore minimal clothing typical of early Mycenaean warriors, consisting of a cloth kilt-like garment and bare upper body.

Later chariotry

As with all of the other Mycenaean troop types, in the later period the Mycenaean chariot became lighter and more mobile. The previous heavy box chariot and dual chariot gave way to the light rail chariot, which appeared in the 13th century BC.

The appearance of this new style of chariot accompanied a major change in the tactical role of Mycenaean chariotry. Unlike in the early period, chariot-borne warriors were now expected to dismount to fight, making them in effect mounted infantry. This can be seen by their equipment, which became the same as that of the infantry – a short spear, helmet, body armour, kilt, greaves, and a round shield. A fresco from Pylos also shows a somewhat lighter chariot-borne warrior who wears the cloth tunic in place of body armour. These changes reflect the more mobile nature of warfare in the later period. Such a force would have been useful for rushing troops to areas which had come under sudden attack, as well as for launching such attacks.

CAVALRY

The troop type for which there is the least evidence is cavalry, of which our knowledge is limited to what can be gleaned from a handful of pottery fragments. These date to the end of the Mycenaean period, giving some indication of the spread of the art of horse-riding to Greece. As regards dress, one relatively detailed depiction from Mycenae shows the cavalryman wearing greaves, the familiar late period tunic, and what appears to be upper-body armour. Stirrups were as yet unknown, saddlery being in its infancy. The horse was fitted with a saddle probably consisting of little more than a padded blanket. The reins and bridle were probably relatively developed owing to the long tradition of chariotry in Mycenaean Greece. Examples of bits have been found, although whether they come from saddle horses or chariot horses is unknown.

The role of saddle horses in Mycenaean warfare is a matter for conjecture, since no depictions or descriptions of combat involving cavalry are known. No weapons can be seen in the few depictions. Although this might be taken as evidence that these warriors did not carry spears or javelins, it cannot be said for sure that they were not armed with swords. Due to the highly stylized and fragmentary nature of the pictorial evidence, as well as the unfamiliar subject for the artist, the sword may have been omitted as it was hidden by the figure's right side (the depictions show the figures facing to their left).

If they did carry a sword, it is possible that these warriors fought as cavalry. However, it is equally possible that the warriors shown mounted represent a class who, although not rich or prestigious enough to own a chariot, could afford a horse to carry them around rather than walking. The third possibility is that these warriors constituted a force of mounted infantry. This would tie in to the evidence that some chariots in the later period were also designed simply for swift transport. Such a force would have been particularly suited to responding to the kind of raids that seem to have been occurring in the later period.

MILITARY ORGANIZATION

The Mycenaean army was not composed of a horde of individual noble warriors who dressed and armed themselves however they liked. Instead, the literary and archaeological evidence shows that it was composed of several well organized and equipped troop types, each with their own characteristic formations and tactical uses. These troops were organized into units of those similarly equipped, and must therefore have been 'drilled' at least to some extent. In this respect Mycenaean armies were similar to those of more imperialist contemporaries such as the Hittites and Egyptians. A degree of organization was clearly necessary to a military culture which retained power in its own homelands for centuries, and seized and controlled other areas such as the Aegean islands and Crete. Therefore, it follows that each Mycenaean army would need to be supported by a command and logistics system equally well developed, by the standards of its age. This issue has been more fully addressed in the previous Mycenaean scholarship.

The most useful primary evidence of Mycenaean organization comes from the Pylos and Knossos Linear B tablets. Some information about

Mycenaean military leadership can also be gleaned from depictions. The late 13th century BC Pylos tablets provide us with a great deal of information on this topic. Although Mycenaean tactical doctrine appears to have undergone a significant change in the 13th century BC, such aspects as higher command structure and logistics may be presumed to have remained relatively unchanged from the earlier period, at least as far as they seem to fit the other evidence. The Linear B archives paint a picture of a highly developed bureaucracy dealing with military matters. This in itself suggests that the Mycenaean army must have been well organized and institutionalized to warrant such a palace bureaucracy to support it. The relevant tablets deal with such things as unit composition, deployments, garrisons, equipping of troops, and supplies.

Battlefield organization

The Mycenaean military system was composed of many units of various troop types which had to work in conjunction with one another on the battlefield in order to fulfil their various tactical roles. In the classic field battle the heavy infantry which seem to have formed the core of the army would have been drawn up in line in the centre. The heavy infantry would most likely have been organized into a number of units within the main battle line, for reasons of command and control. Because swordsmen seem to have fought closely with and against heavy infantry, units of such lighter troops were probably deployed amongst the heavy infantry units or

The 'Lion Gate' at Mycenae. This was the main entrance to the citadel, of which the massive stone circuit walls were built in the 13th century BC. The sculpture above the gate may have been the city's or ruler's badge. (George Mylonas, *Mycenae and the Mycenaean Age*, © 1966 Princeton University Press; reprinted by permission of Princeton University Press)

around them. On the flanks of the main battle line would have been other light infantry such as javelinmen and more swordsmen. The skirmishers, being screening troops by nature, would have been deployed in their loose formations across the front of the army, from where they could screen the troops behind them from opposing missile fire and harass the enemy with their own arrows and sling bullets.

The heavy chariotry of the earlier period, also organized into one or more units (depending on how many were fielded), could conceivably have been deployed in any of three ways: either in front of the heavy infantry, behind them, or on the flanks. The first would have allowed the chariots to charge directly into either the enemy chariots or heavy infantry. This does not seem likely, since it would involve charging frontally against well ordered spearmen or chariots. Chariots seem to have been most effective against disordered or outflanked troops – the Hittites and even the approximately contemporary Chinese used them in this way.

If the chariots were deployed behind the main battle line they could have been used to deliver the *coup de grace* after the heavy infantry and swordsmen had done their work of breaking up and disordering the enemy line. There is a problem with this, however: how would friendly infantry be able to get out of the way of their own chariots charging from behind them? On the other hand, should friendly infantry put their opponents to flight and create a gap for their chariots, the latter would have been very useful for pursuing the fleeing foot.

The third possibility, that of the chariots being deployed on one or both of the flanks, would have given them the opportunity to defeat the enemy's flank troops and turn the flank of his main battle line. This therefore seems the most probable use of heavy chariots in tactical warfare. Indeed, at the battle of Kadesh (1300 BC) the Hittite chariots struck the first blow of the battle by charging the unguarded flank of one of the Egyptian divisions.

The point of these speculations is to give an appreciation of why the Mycenaean army would have required an organized command structure in order to get their various troop types to work together as an army. Certain functional appointments would have been unavoidable: there must have been a commander-in-chief, and at least one officer for every unit in the army. The commander-in-chief's job would be, presumably, to plan the routes of march of an army on campaign, and to devise the plan of attack once the battlefield had been chosen (as well as take the credit for victory and the blame for defeat, no doubt). He would give these orders to the unit commanders, who in turn would order their units to move in accordance with the plan and some required timetable.

Command structure

The highest rank in the Mycenaean army was most likely the *wanax* (chief) of one of the rich palaces such as Mycenae, Knossos, etc. Although we know practically nothing about the *wanakae* except from the tablets that record their privileges, and Homer, who might have preserved their names, they were probably the 'owners' of the forces in their region. The rich burials of the Mycenaeans are generally accepted to be those of the highest level of society, and the grave goods in many of these paint a picture of a militaristic ruling class. Heads of state were the usual commanders-in-chief of most ancient armies, including those of the contemporary Egyptians and Hittites. This was natural, since they had to be seen as military leaders who could protect their people. Homer tells us that for the Trojan expedition the many Achaean kingdoms were united in a confederacy led by the king of Mycenae. However, even if this confederacy is not a fiction but a piece of history which survived through the oral tradition down to Homer's day, it probably dates to at least the late 13th century BC – quite late in the Mycenaean chronology. The uniformity of military dress and equipment in Mycenaean Greece, Crete and the Aegean in general does not necessarily imply that there was one city or king controlling all of it; rather, it suggests a common Achaean mode of warfare.

It is possible that alliances and pacts were formed between palaces, as seen in the mainland's control of Knossos. Mycenaean Greece was made up of small autonomous states ruled by independent chiefs. There may have been family ties between them, but nothing definite is known about the relationship of one settlement to another. Given a good set of rich graves, like those of Mycenae, at other sites, it might have been possible to extrapolate the relative wealth of these settlements and therefore their relative power, but unfortunately this is not the case. The evidence at Mycenae is largely missing and all of its *tholoi* (a type of tomb) have been looted. The fact that the finest array of military equipment of the period was found at Dendra is simply a matter of chance, and tells us nothing about the ranking of Argolid sites. These states may have had loose military associations at one time or another, which may be the origin of Homer's idea of a confederacy; but it must be imagined that over centuries such alliances would sometimes have broken down, resulting in inter-state wars and the rearrangements of such relationships.

The *wanax* probably held supreme authority over the fighting forces and came from the highest class of society. His immediate deputy was the *lawakete* (or *eqeta*), translated as 'leader of the fighting people'. This purely military figure was probably the real 'brains' behind the army's strategy and tactics, since he was free of the much broader concerns of the *wanax*. He would presumably have been of high birth to entitle him to hold such an important position, and might well have been a member of the *wanax*'s family.

Below these leaders of the state the 'regimental' commanders and the *basileis* must have operated. The *basileis* included administrators of provincial estates, whom we find being given new land in the Pylos tablets. Due to the expense and prestige of chariots, the warriors who were mounted on them were probably from the upper class of society. This could include landowners such as *basileis* and other high-born and therefore wealthy men. The palace served as the administrative, command and supply centre of the army. Chariot units were organized and controlled by the palace, as the tablets show.

Higher organization: the evidence and the arguments
The role of the palace as the 'general headquarters' of the Mycenaean army, issuing detailed orders for the deployment of troops, can be seen in the Pylos tablets of the 13th century BC, and may perhaps be presumed for the earlier period. The tablets record the installation at

several places along the Messenian coast of bodies of troops each consisting of a commander, several officers and a number of soldiers. Each contingent is accompanied by a nobleman with the title *eqeta*. Some have interpreted the *eqeta* as a kind of liaison officer between the field unit and the palace, others as the commander of a regiment of the army. Since each group lists an officer as well as an *eqeta*, the former interpretation seems more likely.

This document, comprising five tablets, is headed 'Thus the watchers are guarding the coastal regions'. It tells us that Pylos, being an unwalled coastal city, feared an attack from the sea, and that the authorities at the palace decided to send out small units to watch for raids. The whole coast was divided into ten sectors; the name of the official responsible for each sector is listed, followed by a few other names who are presumably his subordinate officers. In a world without maps, this shows a high level of organization.

The palace bureaucracy also records the issue of what appears to be clothing to be distributed to the *eqeta* and *keseno* (see below) at Knossos. These documents form part of a series of tablets that deal with a specific kind of textile or garment called *pawea*. This garment/textile is further defined by adjectives such as *peneweta* ('with wedge pattern'), *aroa* ('of better quality'), *reukonuku* ('with white fringes'), *eutarapi* ('with red pattern'), and others. It has already been suggested that the *eqetae* were high-ranking commanders. *Keseno*, on the other hand, seem to have been a sort of alternative to the *eqetae* but of a lower rank, since they are never issued with garments 'of better quality', but with those of rather uniform decoration. It is likely that the word *keseno* was the designation for foreign warriors who were supplied with garments from the palace. This is supported by the Captain of the Blacks fresco from Knossos, which shows the Nubian warrior wearing the same type of wedge-patterned Mycenaean kilt as his Greek leader. Finally, the total amount of stored *pawea* was probably about 453 items, the large number being an indication that we are dealing with uniforms.

A Mycenaean army composed of most or all of the different troop types identified here would have consisted of several thousand soldiers of all ranks. Because of this, it is impossible that its warriors could all have been drawn from the local region's ruling elite. Some disagree with this, believing that the Mycenaean soldier was first represented by the individual aristocrat from the time of the Shaft Graves, followed by an elite corps at the time of the fall of Knossos, and that it was not until the 13th century BC that units of common men developed, trained to fight on foot and led by horse-taming officers. However, this model is unlikely to be accurate. It sounds heavily influenced by the Homeric 'heroizing' of Mycenaean warriors and Homer's picture of individualistic warfare. Could the individual aristocrat of the 16th century BC have exerted enough power over the population of his region to control them, interact with far-off kingdoms, and retain his position, without an actual army behind him? As for the suggestion that the individual aristocratic warriors had developed into an elite corps by the time of the fall of Knossos (c.1400 BC), it has since been shown that although the graves of this period do seem to represent part of an 'aristocracy', the exclusively military character of such a class cannot be demonstrated.

Although it is probably correct that in the 13th century BC soldiers were organized into units of trained common men, the evidence suggests that this was also being done as early as the Shaft Grave period (c.1650–1550 BC). The main evidence for this is the depictions and finds of weapons in the Shaft Graves associated with, for example, the employment of units of heavy spearmen.

Driessen and Macdonald analysed the so-called 'Warrior Graves' of c.1450–1400 BC Crete to see what they could tell us about Knossian military organization in the Mycenaean period. They started with the assumption that, given the evidence for a centralized society and bureaucracy, a military organization was likely to have been part of the palace structure. It does not seem likely that there was a specific 'warrior class' within Knossian society, such as the later *homoioi* of Sparta. The most plausible interpretation of these graves is that they represent officials of different ranks in the palace military organization. These warriors may have been drawn from different levels of society, though the wealth of their graves suggests that all of them were from the upper levels. The Knossos graves furnished with swords are not poor burials, and none are likely to represent the lower classes or the rank and file of the Knossian army.

As to whether this kind of military organization was also present in other areas of the Aegean, Driessen and Macdonald say that it was possibly unique to Knossos at the turn of the 15th century BC. Although lack of evidence from the mainland prevents firm comparisons between mainland sites and Crete, such uniqueness does not seem likely, given the facts that at this time Knossos had been taken over by the Mycenaeans, and the language in which this 'Knossian' bureaucracy was being conducted was an early form of Greek.

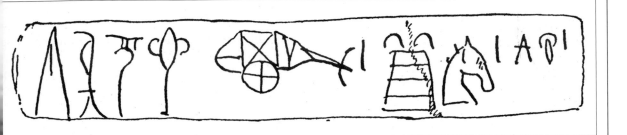

Although the evidence for an institutionalized military organization on the mainland is not at all conclusive, the fact that such an organization was set up at Knossos under Mycenaean control, in their language, allows a confident inference that such a level of organization also existed on the mainland. There is also the argument from need: such an organization would be necessary to equip, train and command armies like those of Knossos and Pylos – armies of several thousand soldiers, organized into like-armed units of various types.

This prompts the question, who made up the rank and file of the Mycenaean army? If some (probably most) of these soldiers were drawn from the common folk of a given region, it would have been necessary for the 'state' (centred on the palace) to arrange for hundreds of shields and weapons to be made and issued to the recruits. In order for a unit of Mycenaean heavy infantry to perform its tactical role effectively its shields would all have to be of a relatively uniform size and its spears of the same length. This is certainly the case with the 16th century BC warriors depicted in a fresco from Akrotiri on Thera (the present day Aegean island of Santorini), as well as for the Knossian depictions of light infantry, and the heavy infantrymen shown on the earlier Siege Rhyton. In addition to arming and equipping such a force, the state would have to organize the training of the soldiers according to their particular troop type, to fight in appropriate formations and to manoeuvre without falling into disorder. In short, they would have to be drilled, and in order to achieve this a well organized military system would have to be in place.

Returning to the question of whether or not such a military organization existed in other Mycenaean centres besides Knossos, the archaeological record of Mycenaean plate armour may also be significant. At Knossos we have documents listing the issue of corselets, but no archaeological evidence. At nine other Mycenaean sites we have archaeological evidence of corselets, but no documentary evidence. Knossos tells us that these corselets were dealt with by the palace bureaucracy, even though none may have actually survived from there. It is therefore reasonable to suppose that, having the actual remains of corselets at other sites, these too would originally have been issued by the local palace. After all, as has been seen, these corselets were used by expensive chariot-borne soldiers, and would themselves have been difficult and expensive to make.

One characteristic of the Mycenaean army compared to that of the contemporary Egyptians or Hittites is that the formers' equipment is comparatively less uniform. It may be that different palaces had slightly different patterns of shields, helmets, etc, which in turn suggests a number of highly centralized states.

Linear B tablet from Mycenaean Knossos, one of the many that deal with military equipment. This particular example records the issue to a warrior of a dual chariot, an armoured corselet and horses. (After Palmer, 1965)

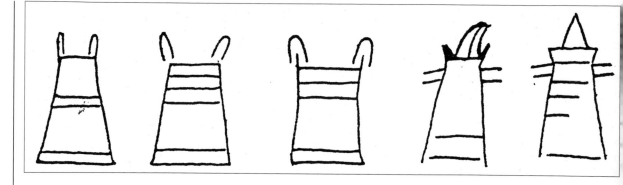

Linear B ideograms of corselets from Knossos and Pylos. These come from tablets recording the allocation of military equipment to warriors, and are evidence of a well-developed Mycenaean military organization. (After Ventris & Chadwick)

The breeding or importing of hundreds of horses to draw chariots, as well as the actual training of these horses (a highly expensive and specialized skill), would likewise need to be organized under some central authority. Evidence for the allocation of chariot horses can be found in the Knossos tablets, which show horses itemized alongside corselets and wheeled chariots, together with a man's name. There are about 11 entries with 'a single horse', and at least 25 with 'a pair of horses'. This small number of listed horse teams, as compared to the overall listing of 400-plus chariots, might be explained by the simple possibility that most of the tablets recording horses did not survive the destruction of the palace – such survivals are, by definition, random. We know from depictions that the chariots had a team of two horses, so why were some men only issued with one? The answer could lie in the fact that the same applies with regard to the issue of corselets. A possible explanation is that this set of tablets are 'tying up the loose ends' in the general equipping of the Knossian chariot corps. The fact that in some cases a bronze ingot ideogram – enough for a pair of corselets – is inserted instead is also in keeping with this interpretation.

Unit sizes

It was the usual practice in organized ancient armies to have at least a nominal or suggested set of unit strengths. It is not easy to reconstruct normal unit sizes for any of the known Mycenaean troop types, but what little evidence can be gleaned from the Pylos Linear B tablets of c.1300 BC is quite interesting. These troops were always divided into multiples of ten, so it appears that they organized their units based on the decimal system. It is likely that at the time of the Pylos tablets the actual strengths of various types of units differed from those of the earlier periods before the implied change in methods of warfare. However, the fact that the army (and hence the palace military organization) used the decimal system is something so fundamental and remote from tactics that there is no reason to doubt that it also applied earlier.

Interestingly, use of the decimal system for unit organization seems to have been common in Bronze Age armies. As a contemporary example, the Hittites had officers in charge of 1,000 and 10,000 men in a rising hierarchy of command. Even the *Tai Kung's Six Secret Teachings*, an ancient Chinese book on the art of war, states: 'For the chariots – a leader for five chariots, a captain for fifteen, a commander for fifty, and a general for one hundred.' Admittedly, this book's current recension probably dates to many centuries after the Late Bronze Age; but it nonetheless contains concepts originating early in the era of Chinese chariot warfare.

In conclusion, although we may never have any hard evidence for the size and organization of early Mycenaean units, it does seem likely that they were based on the decimal system and that there was a rising hierarchy of command, with each higher rank commanding a greater number of soldiers. On a purely practical level, this is the most efficient way to organize and command an army; a 'pyramidal' structure is the norm in any multi-class state or bureaucracy, and is thus in keeping with what we know of the structure of Mycenaean society.

Issues of equipment

The warrior graves with their weapons, armour and wealth, and the titles of the Linear B documents, show us something of the upper classes of the Mycenaean army who would have provided the chariot corps and the officers; but what of the rank and file?

It is unlikely that common soldiers would be identifiable as such in the graves. The burials furnished with swords (i.e. the Warrior Graves at Knossos) are not those of poor men. The rank-and-file was probably composed of the common people who made up the great majority of the population of any Aegean kingdom. Most would be unable to afford the necessary equipment, but all were necessary to make up the numbers of any army. Therefore their weapons, shields and helmets would have to be paid for by the state, and would probably have 'remained the property of...' whichever palace supplied them. (This would also ensure the necessary uniformity of equipment.) This seems even to have been the case to some extent for the upper class of soldiers, since some of their equipment (e.g. corselets) is also listed in the palace archives, which suggests that the palace owned it and was issuing it. If equipment was centrally provided, it is logical that a common soldier would not be at liberty to have his military panoply buried with him; in such systems it would be normal for it to be stored in the palace arsenal. This may explain why the majority of the soldiers of the Mycenaean army are not visible in the archaeological record.

The palace seems to have been the centre of production of weapons for the military. The evidence for this comes mostly from the Knossos tablets, but also from archaeological finds. We have evidence for the production and inventory of arrowheads, spearheads, javelinheads and swords, thus broadly covering the weaponry for all the known troop types with the exception of slingers. (The absence of sling ammunition from inventories and graves hardly weighs against the general argument, however. Slingers were, after all, probably loosely organized and locally raised irregulars, and they may well have continued to use the earlier unfired clay or knapped stone projectiles rather than cast lead bullets like the later Greek and Roman *glandes*.)

As for the other types of light infantry and skirmishers, i.e. archers, javelinmen and swordsmen, the fact that their weapons were made of bronze meant that the palace did direct their production. Turning again to the Knossos tablets, Sir Arthur Evans found a cache of tablets which show ideograms of what appear to be swords; a tablet serving as a total to this series lists some 50 of these. This relatively small number has been suggested to be an inventory of the equipment of a ruler's bodyguard; but once again, it should be stressed that the scarcity of any item in the archaeological record is not in itself a 'proof of a negative'. It is noteworthy that the number of swords listed supports the evidence that Mycenaean units were organized in multiples of ten. Although it seems that in general the palace may have issued swords to soldiers, their presence in elite burials suggests that those who were wealthy enough to provide their own arms did so.

The Knossos tablets also list numbers of javelins and arrows. Evans found some seal impressions with the word *pataja* and an ideogram of a short pointed stick, and in association with these, finds that he described as arrowheads. It was therefore initially thought that *pataja* meant arrows. However, there is another ideogram with flights on the tail which looks more like an arrow, so the pointed stick labelled *pataja* is more probably a light javelin. This is significant because it ties in with the depictions of warriors armed with such weapons, notably the Captain of the Blacks and Warriors Hurling Javelins frescoes. It also shows that the palace equipped these troop types.

Not surprisingly, in addition to light infantry and skirmisher weapons, the Knossos tablets show that the palace controlled the supply of the heavy infantry's main arm, the large spear. This is clearly what is called *enkhos* on the tablets – the same word as in the Classical period.

Finally, turning to the archaeological evidence, fragments of swords were actually found in the same corridor at Knossos as the clay Linear B seal impressions which listed swords. The most indisputable evidence that the palace stored weapons in bulk comes from the 'Armoury' at Knossos, where three seal impressions were found attached to the charred remains of two wooden boxes containing carbonized arrow shafts and arrowheads. In the same building was found a tablet with the arrow symbol followed by the high numbers 6,010 and 2,630.

SELECT BIBLIOGRAPHY

The following are some of the main sources which have proved useful in the research for this book:

Anderson, J.K., 'Greek Chariot-Borne and Mounted Infantry', *American Journal of Archaeology* 79:175–187 (1975)

Astrom, P., *The Cuirass Tomb and Other Finds at Dendra* (Goeteborg, 1977)

Buchholz, H.G., & V.Karageorghis, *Prehistoric Greece and Cyprus* (London, 1973)

Chadwick, J., *The Mycenaean World* (Cambridge, 1980)

Driessen, J.M., & C.Macdonald, 'Some Military Aspects of the Aegean in the Late Fifteenth and Early Fourteenth Centuries BC', *Annual of the British School at Athens* 79:49–74 (1984)

Evans, A.J., *The Annual of the British School at Athens, No.IV, Session 1899–1900* 48:110–113 (London, 1900)

The Annual of the British School at Athens, No.VI, Session 1899–1900 48 (London, 1900)

Greenhalgh, P.A.L., 'The Dendra Charioteer', *Antiquity* 54:210–5 (1980)

Early Greek Warfare: Horsemen and Chariots in the Homeric and Archaic Ages (Cambridge, 1973)

Lang, M., *The Palace of Nestor at Pylos in Western Messenia,* vol.2,
    The Frescoes (Princeton, 1969)

Littauer, M., & J.H.Crouwel, 'Chariots in Late Bronze Age Greece',
    Antiquity 57:187–92 (1983)

Manning, S.W., 'The Military Function in Late Minoan I Crete: a note',
    World Archaeology 18, volume 2: 284–88 (Cambridge, 1986)

Matz, F., *Crete and Early Greece, The Prelude to Greek Art* (Holland, 1962)

Miller, R., McEwen, E., & C.Bergman, 'Experimental Approaches to
    Ancient Near Eastern Archery', *World Archaeology 18, volume 2:*
    179–95 (Cambridge, 1986)

Ministry of Culture – The National Hellenic Committee – ICOM, *The
    Mycenaean World, Five Centuries of Early Greek Culture 1600–1100 BC*
    (Athens, 1988)

Moorey, P.R.S., 'The Emergence of the Light, Horse-Drawn Chariot
    in the Near East c.2000–1500 BC', *World Archaeology 18, volume 2:*
    197–215 (Cambridge, 1986)

Powell, T.G.E., 'Some Implications of Chariotry', in *Culture and
    Environment. Essays in Honour of Sir Cyril Fox,* ed. I.Foster &
    L.Adcock, 153–69 (London, 1963)

Schliemann, H., *Mycenae; A Narrative of Researches and Discoveries
    at Mycenae and Tiryns* (London, 1878)

Schuchhardt, C., *Schliemann's Excavations, An Archaeological and
    Historical Study* (New York, 1971)

Taylour, W.D., *The Mycenaeans* (New York, 1964)

Thurston, S., 'LBA Chariot Warfare – Part II', *www.LivingHistory.co.uk
    (1100–1500 Articles and Resources)* (1999)

Ventris, M., & J.Chadwick, *Documents in Mycenaean Greek*
    (Cambridge, 1973)

Vermeule, E., *Greece in the Bronze Age* (London, 1972)

Wees, H. van, 'Kings in Combat: Battles and Heroes in the Iliad',
    Classical Quarterly 38: 1–24 (1988)

Weingartner, S., 'In the Near Eastern Bronze Age, chariot tactics were
    more sophisticated than previously supposed', *Military Heritage,*
    August 2002: 18–22, 79 (USA, 2002)

THE PLATES

A: EARLY INFANTRY, c.1500 BC

The inspiration for this scene was taken from a seal found in Shaft Grave III at Mycenae. It shows a very lightly attired swordsman stabbing a heavy spearman in the throat over the rim of the latter's figure-of-eight shield, having got past the point of his long and unwieldy spear. The Theran heavy spearman (A1) has been added.

A1: Theran heavy spearman

This warrior is one of a row of spearmen seen on a fresco from Akrotiri, Thera (on the present-day Aegean island of Santorini). Akrotiri is known as the 'Pompeii of the Bronze Age', having been entombed in volcanic ash after the island literally exploded in around 1500 BC. His helmet, of leather faced with sliced boar's tusks, is plumed; it is not known what colour Mycenaean plumes were, or whether their colour was related to any organizational system. He has a simple, probably early-pattern of 'tower' shield, carried – or rather worn – by means of a leather strap (*telamon*) which passes over his left shoulder and under his right arm. His ashwood spear is tipped with a 'shoe-socketed' bronze head, this also being of an early design. The fresco from which he comes is unique in that it actually shows the spearmen's swords, in leather scabbards with decorative tassels.

A2: Swordsman

This fierce character may be represented as a member of something of an elite, perhaps even similar in temperament to the Viking 'berserker'. These unprotected swordsmen were apparently regarded as very brave; apart from attacking heavy infantry, as here, there are several depictions in Mycenaean art of this type of warrior fighting a lion. His 'horned' sword is carried in an unusually ornate scabbard.

A3: Heavy spearman

This warrior wears the uniquely Aegean figure-of-eight shield, so named for its shape, and made from wickerwork on a wooden frame, covered with cowhide, and with a raised boss-like central rib. Like all early Mycenaean heavy infantry shields, this type was worn by means of a *telamon*.

He too wears the characteristically Aegean 'boar's-tusk' helmet. His spear had the socketed spearhead which was a development of the earlier shoe- or double-socketed type.

B: EARLY INFANTRY, 16th–15th CENTURIES BC

This scene is inspired by one found on a decorative gold ring from Mycenae, now called 'The Battle in the Glen' ring, and dated to the 16th century BC. On the ring the dagger-armed warrior is portrayed as the 'hero' of the scene, slaying another swordsman and rescuing an unarmed man. For the sake of variety the second swordsman has been replaced here by a javelinman, and a heavy spearman looks on; perhaps they belong to a defeated and fleeing army.

B1: Light infantry swordsman, 16th century BC

This heroic warrior is armed with a type of triangular dagger found in large numbers on Crete. He wears the minimal clothing characteristic of early light infantry. The fact that he has a boar's-tusk helmet is not unusual: most swordsmen found in depictions are so equipped. This and the prominence with which they are portrayed suggest that such light troops were held in relatively high regard, possibly due to the dangerous and individualistic nature of their tactical role.

B2: Creto-Mycenaean javelinman, c.1450 BC

This figure is taken from an obscure fragment of fresco found in Mycenaean Knossos, and named by its discoverer, Sir Arthur Evans, 'Warriors Hurling Javelins'. It depicts a dense mass of these javelinmen launching their weapons high into the air. This skirmisher wears a white neck band, apparently a characteristic of Mycenaean javelinmen – it may even have been a badge of their troop type.

B3: Heavy spearman, 16th century BC

This warrior carries the fully developed pattern of tower shield, of curved section and shaped into a raised neck guard on the top rim. The carrying strap allowed the shield's

Seal impression from Mycenae, 16th century BC, showing a light swordsman dispatching a heavy spearman – see Plate A. This scene is significant because it gives an insight into one of the tactical uses of such swordsmen, to break up heavy spear formations using their greater agility. (Courtesy Professor Dr H-G.Buchholz)

position to be changed from the front to the back of the body by throwing the upper body and shoulders back or forward as needed. Like all early period spearmen he is equipped with a boar's-tusk helmet. His spearhead is of the 'slit-socketed' type, a transitional design between the shoe-socketed and fully socketed types.

C: EARLY MISSILE TROOPS, 16th–15th CENTURIES BC

This scene shows three distinct kinds of light troops employed by the early Mycenaeans, and the three missile weapons used. As well as battlefield skirmishers, such troops would have been far more suited to the defence of citadel walls than heavy spearmen or swordsmen.

C1: Regular archer, 16th century BC

This archer can be found on a scene inlaid into the blade of a dagger from one of the Shaft Graves at Mycenae. He is shown supporting heavy spearmen, fighting an enemy portrayed as lions. Our description of this archer as a 'regular' is a relative term, in that he is not nude like some other depictions of Mycenaean archers, but wears a garment decorated in the same way as those of his four comrades on the inlaid scene, suggesting uniform regularity. He is armed with a composite bow which when drawn assumes a semi-circular shape. His arrowhead is made of knapped obsidian (volcanic glass); at a time when bronze was still expensive this material provided a cheap and expendable alternative. The number found in elite burials indicates that their use was not restricted to the lower classes.

C2: Irregular slinger, 16th century BC

This figure represents what was probably the lowest class of Mycenaean warrior. He comes from an embossed silver *rhyton* (a vessel used to pour libations) now called the 'Siege Rhyton', which depicts an assault on a walled town. The naked slingers and archers are shown skirmishing ahead of heavy spearmen with tower shields. Slingers such as this one may have been civilians who were called out to defend their town if it came under attack. His weapon is cheap and simple, being nothing more than a piece of leather cut to shape. His projectile is made of unfired clay and is based on earlier excavated examples; these sling bullets were also made of shaped stones.

C3: Nubian mercenary javelinman, 1450–1400 BC

Taken from a fresco found in Mycenaean Knossos and called 'The Captain of the Blacks', this figure portrays a foreign mercenary in Mycenaean service. The fresco shows what was evidently a line of African warriors led by a Greek officer. The two feathers fixed into his hair suggest that he is Nubian; this type of adornment can also be seen in Egyptian depictions of Nubians, who were regarded as excellent light troops. He carries two light javelins with heads cut from bronze plate and tangs driven into the end of the shafts. His garment is relatively ornate, which may suggest this was one of the palace's élite specialist units. As well as the characteristic javelinman's neck band he wears two bronze rings above each ankle, which may or may not be a Nubian element.

D: DUAL CHARIOT, 1500–1400 BC

Inspired by a scene carved on a gravestone from Mycenae, this plate depicts the heavy 'dual chariot' of the earlier period, so named because the cab is of dual construction,

incorporating the box proper and semi-circular 'wings' projecting from the rear sides. Except for the mouth bits of the bridle, no remains of Mycenaean chariots have been found, so reconstructions can only be made by studying depictions and texts as well as making comparisons with surviving Egyptian chariots. The braced double draught pole appears to be a strengthening feature of the Aegean chariot. We do know that the chariots stored at Mycenaean Knossos were painted various shades of red, and that those probably used by higher ranks were inlaid with ivory.

D1: Warrior in corselet, c.1400 BC

This warrior wears the famous 'Dendra panoply' named after the site of its discovery. This remarkable suit of bronze armour is the most complete example found of the type of corselets issued to chariot-borne warriors in the Linear B tablets, but fragments of a number of similar armours have been found elsewhere. The various plates were joined together by leather thongs and designed to be able to slide over each other, allowing the wearer enough movement to wield his long spear effectively. The boar's-tusk helmet and arm guards were also found with the corselet.

D2: Charioteer, 15th century BC

Unlike the warrior, the chariot driver was not expected to engage in combat; his job was to maintain control of the chariot and manoeuvre it into position for the warrior to use his spear. This would have taken great skill, given the relative heaviness of these early chariots and the rocky Greek terrain. For this reason he wears only a waist garment and a boar's-tusk helmet like that of his comrade, with bronze cheek guards and plume.

D3: Swordsman, 15th century BC

Although evidently highly effective against disordered bodies of heavy infantry, a loosely formed unit of light swordsmen would probably have been vulnerable to a chariot attack. His weapon is a long thrusting sword (sometimes called a 'rapier'), of which many examples have been found.

E: LATER INFANTRY, c.1250–1200 BC

These figures are taken from those portrayed on the 'Warrior Vase' found at Mycenae, and a fresco fragment from the palace at Pylos. These palaces were destroyed in the late 13th century BC, so these finds can be dated to that period. They show a major change in Mycenaean military dress and equipment from the earlier period, and imply a corresponding change in tactics.

E1: Mycenaean spearman

Taken from the Warrior Vase, this man wears the so-called 'horned helmet'. We interpret this as being made from hardened leather with bronze studs added for extra strength; it is adorned with two 'horns' – probably tusks from a boar – and a plume mounted in a raised comb. His torso is well protected by a simple front-and-back bronze cuirass; his 'kilt' is also for protection, being made of leather with bronze studs. Underneath his greaves he wears woollen over-the-knee socks. The small bag attached to his spear is used for carrying the warrior's rations and personal belongings on the march.

E2: Mycenaean spearman

This warrior comes from the opposite side of the Warrior Vase to E1. He is dressed and equipped the same as his comrade, apart from his headgear, of the type now known as the 'hedgehog helmet'. This seems to have been

This fresco from Mycenae clearly shows the curved rim, longitudinal rib boss and cowhide covering of the figure-of-eight shield, the cowhide painted with dark brown patches on a white background. This depiction is dated to the 13th century, when such shields were no longer in use. (Courtesy National Archaeological Museum, Athens)

constructed from or covered with the spined pelts of actual hedgehogs, attached to a leather frame. Such a helmet appears elsewhere in depictions of later Mycenaean warriors, and apparently denotes a separate unit from those wearing the horned helmet. Both these warriors carry slung on their backs 'inverted *pelta*' shields. This type probably also had handles for carrying it on the arm when fighting, though none can be seen in depictions.

E3: Pylian infantryman

This fallen warrior comes from the fresco fragment from the palace at Pylos. His dress is characteristically Pylian, namely the linen tunic and thick fabric greaves. It is unclear from the fresco whether his weapon is a javelin intended for throwing or a spear for thrusting. In any case he appears to be a medium infantryman, owing to the fact that he has armour in the form of a shield and greaves but no body armour.

F: PYLIAN LIGHT INFANTRY AND 'BARBARIANS', c.1250–1200 BC

Among the fresco fragments found at the site of the palace at Pylos was one showing a skirmish between soldiers and what can only be described as 'savages' or barbarians, which is the inspiration for this plate.

F1: Light spearman

Confirmation that this warrior's weapon is intended for thrusting rather than throwing is provided by the fresco, where one can be seen being thrust into a barbarian's groin. His secondary weapon is a sword slung from a shoulder belt. He is very lightly attired, with only a linen kilt with leather overlay and linen greaves. This would have made him well suited for operations in the rough fringes of Mycenaean rule, where the barbarians dwelt.

F2: Swordsman

This warrior is possibly from the same unit as his comrade F1, owing to their identical dress; however, there is no indication that he too carried a spear. His sword is of the type known as 'cruciform-shouldered'. His boar's-tusk helmet is in its fully evolved form, with a curved neck guard and small tusk crest.

F3: 'Barbarian'

This savage hillman uses a Mycenaean sword taken from a slain Pylian soldier. His garment is simply a piece of hide or fleece torn so that it can be tied at the shoulder. It is unknown who exactly these warriors represent in the Pylos fresco; however, the thought that they may have had something to do with the city's unexplained destruction is intriguing.

G: RAIL CHARIOT, c.1250–1150 BC

This scene shows the chariot halted beneath the 'Lion Gate' at Mycenae. The pottery fragment from which the chariot and its crew are reconstructed came from the neighbouring palace at Tiryns. Although a major centre in its own right, Tiryns appears to have been politically dominated by Mycenae, and it is from there that the charioteer has travelled. The rail chariot was the last type documented in Bronze Age Greece and, like the dual chariot, was of local origin.

G1: Charioteer

He wears a thick linen corselet over a woollen tunic, and his lower torso is further protected by a padded bronze waist belt held on by its own tension. His conical bronze helmet has cheek guards.

G2: Spearman

This spearman is less well equipped than those shown in Plate E, and may be a levied soldier, owing to his lack of helmet and body armour. He has, however, procured a pair of thin bronze greaves. His round shield and short spear seem to have been typical of the later Mycenaean period.

H1: Mounted warrior, c.1200 BC

Although this rider is probably a cavalryman, it cannot be ruled out that he is a mounted infantryman. Indeed, the vase fragment from which he is reconstructed appears to show him dismounted, although this may be the result of the artist being unfamiliar with the subject matter. His conical bronze helmet has cheek guards attached by leathers, and his cuirass comprises a simple set of breast- and back-plates. Below the edge of his tunic he wears long woollen socks under his thin bronze greaves, and sandals. His weapon is a so-called 'cruciform-hilted rapier'. The tying of the horse's mane in bunches is shown in period sources, but the saddle pad and bridle are conjectural apart from finds of bronze bits.

H2: Mycenaean woman

Offering the warrior a drink of water from a vessel known as a *kylix*, this woman wears the later Mycenaean dress – similar to the men's tunics, but longer. Her hairstyle, with sidelocks and two upwards curls above the forehead, is characteristically Mycenaean, and can be seen in frescoes of the time.

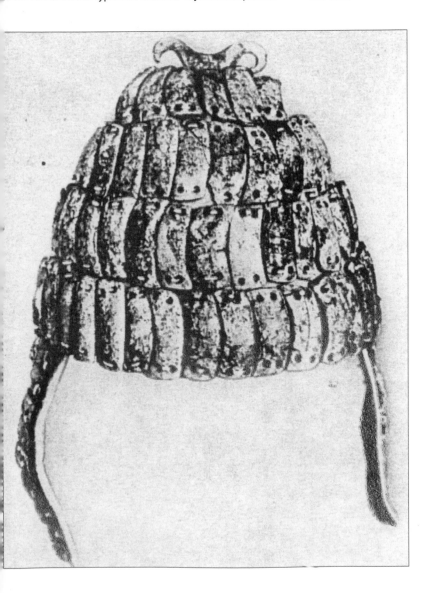

This relatively early example of a boar's-tusk helmet is reconstructed based upon depictions; it dates from between 1550 and 1500 BC and comes from Mycenae itself. Note the cheek guards, also constructed of sliced tusks sewn on to a leather backing. (Courtesy Professor Dr H-G. Buchholz)

INDEX